Opening up

2 Samuel

JIM NEWHEISER

Day One

Opening up

2 Samuel

JIM NEWHEISER

It seems that there is always a shortage of pastors who can faithfully expound God's Word and effectively apply it to people's lives. For this reason, I am profoundly thankful for Jim Newheiser's study on 2 Samuel. Not only does he bring the text to life in new and fresh ways, but also he is always careful to show how each passage finds its ultimate fulfillment in Christ. The study is deep enough for pastors and teachers, and yet accessible enough for every Christian. I highly recommend it.

Michael J. Kruger, President and Professor of New Testament, Reformed Theological Seminary, Charlotte, NC, USA

In this excellent set of biblical studies by Day One, Jim Newheiser has given us yet another fine explanatory commentary, this time on 2 Samuel. We are certainly in his debt already in this series for the very helpful treatment he has given us on the book of Proverbs, and now we are equally encouraged by his Opening Up 2 Samuel. It is filled with wise applications to the believer's life and living, continually focusing our attention on the one to whom the entire Word of God ultimately points: our Lord Jesus Christ. As a busy pastor himself, Newheiser helpfully guides his fellow preachers in how to quickly get to the core meaning of the scriptural text, assisting us in gaining the essential flow of the historical narrative, yet without sacrificing the practical implications for growing Christians. I am thankful for these insightful expositions and pray that they will be read—and heeded—by all who seek to honor Jesus, our sovereign Savior.

Lance Quinn, Founding and Senior Pastor, Thousand Oaks Bible Church, Thousand Oaks, California, USA

This new volume on 2 Samuel by Jim Newheiser is an excellent addition to the "Opening Up" series. The author can always be relied on in the two critical areas that make or break any commentary. The first is biblical accuracy: Newheiser always handles the text with care and integrity. His exposition is driven by what the text says and not by any pre-conceived ideas he may have. The second is application;

too many commentaries give good insight into the meaning of the text but little or no practical application. The reader is left asking "So what?" The reader, in this case, need have no worries on this score either. The writing style is accessible to all. I warmly commend this and Jim Newheiser's other writings; they have a welcome place on my bookshelf.

Colin D. Jones, Pastor, Crawley, UK

Jim Newheiser opens the biblical account of David's reign with clarity, conciseness, exegetical insight, and conscience-searching pastoral wisdom. It is especially helpful that, for every major section of 2 Samuel, he asks both "Where do we see Jesus in this passage?" and "How does this passage apply to us?"—and that he answers them in this order, grounding our response in God's grace in Christ.

Dennis E. Johnson PhD, Professor of Practical Theology, Westminster Seminary California, USA

It is a privilege to read a man's judgments concerning a particular book from the Bible especially when he has been studying that particular Scripture for some years, thought much about it, explained and preached it to an inquiring and discerning congregation, and reacted with them in their questions and observations. He has seen truths that others have not seen. He has seen Christ where others have seen only moral exhortation and judgment and perplexing deaths. But when that book is a neglected part of the Old Testament such as 2 Samuel, when there are few helpful commentaries, then what one is holding in one's hand is a treasure. We are thankful to God for Jim Newheiser's sure guidance through the twenty-four chapters of 2 Samuel.

Geoff Thomas, Pastor, Alfred Place Baptist Church, Aberystwyth, UK

Jim Newheiser has provided us with an extremely useful commentary on 2 Samuel that far outweighs its brevity. The story is summarized with literary skill and insight, making it a delight to read. The shadow of Jesus Christ, whom David images, is constantly pointed out. Practical principles for living are noted, as the author applies God's inspired Word, and the discussion questions will serve to stimulate personal or group study. I highly recommend this commentary for the Christian reader, and especially for preachers of the gospel!

Revd. Bill Green ThM, Executive Secretary, Confraternidad Latinoamericana de Iglesias Reformadas (CLIR), San José, Costa Rica

From the historical account of the good and not-so-good years of David's reign in 2 Samuel, Jim Newheiser highlights the related aspects of Christ's reign over the Christian and, by extension, the church. A vigorous and vivid use of the sacred text.

Hywel R. Jones MA, PhD, Professor Emeritus of Practical Theology, Westminster Seminary California, USA

In a world where heroes frequently fall and those we look up to disappoint us, Jim Newheiser wisely and winsomely guides us to the pedestal of the one Hero who doesn't disappoint. It's not Saul, Samuel, Jonathan, David, or Solomon; the true Hero and Main Character of the Samuel–Kings narratives is God, revealed to us ultimately in His Son, Jesus the Christ. Focusing on 2 Samuel's account of

David's reign, Newheiser offers a theological exposition of David that is sensitive to the flow of the Samuel narratives, the unfolding story of God in the Old Testament, and the glorious fulfillment of these things in the New Testament. Newheiser avoids the pitfall of presenting David as merely a moral example to follow. Instead, while he guides us to see the true greatness of the man, he also brings us to stare at David's sin and folly, so that we may see that ultimately Israel's (and our) longings for the right kind of king must give way to a Greater Son of David—King Jesus.

Dr. Phillip Marshall, Assistant Professor, Department of Classics and Biblical Languages, School of Christian Thought, Houston Baptist University, USA

ISBN 978-1-84625-439-0

British Library Cataloguing in Publication Data available

Published by Day One Publications

Ryelands Road, Leominster, England, HR6 8NZ

TEL 01568 613 740 FAX 01568 611 473

email—sales@dayone.co.uk

UK web site—www.dayone.co.uk

Printed by TJ International

Dedication
With thanks to God for my co-elders at
Grace Bible Church,
who have exemplified the qualities of
Christlike servant-leadership
and have faithfully kept me accountable.
May God help each of us to finish well.

List of Bible abbreviations

		1 Chr.	1 Chronicles	Dan.	Daniel
		2 Chr.	2 Chronicles	Hosea	Hosea
Gen.	Genesis	Ezra	Ezra	Joel	Joel
Exod.	Exodus	Neh.	Nehemiah	Amos	Amos
Lev.	Leviticus	Esth.	Esther	Obad.	Obadiah
Num.	Numbers	Job	Job	Jonah	Jonah
Deut.	Deuteronomy	Ps.	Psalms	Micah	Micah
Josh.	Joshua	Prov.	Proverbs	Nahum	Nahum
Judg.	Judges	Eccles.	Ecclesiastes	Hab.	Habakkuk
Ruth	Ruth	S.of S.	Song of Solomon	Zeph.	Zephaniah
1 Sam.	1 Samuel	Isa.	Isaiah	Hag.	Haggai
2 Sam.	2 Samuel	Jer.	Jeremiah	Zech.	Zechariah
1 Kings	1 Kings	Lam.	Lamentations	Mal.	Malachi
2 Kings	2 Kings	Ezek.	Ezekiel		

		Gal.	Galatians	Heb.	Hebrews
		Eph.	Ephesians	James	James
Matt.	Matthew	Phil.	Philippians	1 Peter	1 Peter
Mark	Mark	Col.	Colossians	2 Peter	2 Peter
Luke	Luke	1 Thes.	1 Thessalonians	1 John	1 John
John	John	2 Thes.	2 Thessalonians	2 John	2 John
Acts	Acts	1 Tim.	1 Timothy	3 John	3 John
Rom.	Romans	2 Tim.	2 Timothy	Jude	Jude
1 Cor.	1 Corinthians	Titus	Titus	Rev.	Revelation
2 Cor.	2 Corinthians	Philem.	Philemon		

Contents

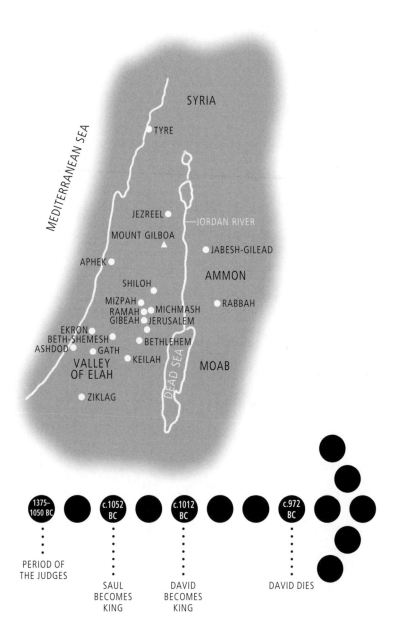

MEDITERRANEAN SEA

SYRIA

TYRE

JEZREEL
JORDAN RIVER
MOUNT GILBOA
JABESH-GILEAD
APHEK
AMMON
SHILOH
MIZPAH
RAMAH   MICHMASH   RABBAH
GIBEAH   JERUSALEM
EKRON
BETH-SHEMESH   BETHLEHEM
ASHDOD   GATH
KEILAH
VALLEY   MOAB
OF ELAH
DEAD SEA
ZIKLAG

| 1375– 1050 BC | | c.1052 BC | | c.1012 BC | | | c.972 BC | | | | | |

PERIOD OF
THE JUDGES

SAUL
BECOMES
KING

DAVID
BECOMES
KING

DAVID DIES

OPENING UP 2 SAMUEL

Background and summary

First and Second Samuel were originally written as one big book. The theme of 1 Samuel was Israel's quest to find a worthy leader. Eli, Samuel, and Saul were unable to meet Israel's need for ongoing godly direction. Then David emerged as the man after God's own heart, who defeated Goliath and who was anointed by God to be a worthy king who would shepherd His people. Saul was jealous and tried to eliminate David. David, on the other hand, refused to take advantage of his opportunities to kill Saul and to seize the kingdom by force as he patiently waited for God's timing for his ascent to the throne. First Samuel ended with the death of Saul at the hands of the Philistines. The way had been cleared for David to reign over his people.

As 2 Samuel begins, the reader has high hopes for an era of great blessing for Israel. Finally a man who is both godly and gifted will rule over God's people. The first ten chapters record David's triumphs as we follow his ascent to the throne and the early years of his reign. He acts with wisdom and honor, treating his former enemies in Israel with grace and conquering the nation's external foes. The climax of the book of 2 Samuel comes in chapter 7, in which God establishes His covenant with David, promising that a Son of David will reign over Israel forever.

But then, when David is at the height of his powers, he commits his great sin with Bathsheba, the wife of Uriah. As a result, chapters 11 through 20 record David's troubles, which come as the consequence of his terrible moral and spiritual failure. One son commits an unspeakable atrocity, while another betrays him. David's kingdom barely survives.

The final four chapters form a kind of epilogue to 2 Samuel in which a few other incidents from David's reign are recorded, and, most importantly, David summarizes God's faithfulness to him in final psalms of praise. One phrase which could summarize the events of David's life as recorded in 2 Samuel is, "As the LORD lives, who has redeemed my life from all distress" (4:9).

How to read and understand 2 Samuel

While we are not certain who wrote 2 Samuel, we know it couldn't have been Samuel because all the events in this book took place after his death. Nor can we be sure when the book was written. Many believe it was written after the division of the kingdom, because there are references to Israel and Judah (1 Sam. 11:8; 17:52; 18:16; 2 Sam. 11:11; 12:8; 19:40–43). We are certain, however, that this book infallibly records the history of Israel. "All Scripture is inspired by God" (2 Tim. 3:16a). We also know that 2 Samuel is not merely a collection of stories about people who lived a long time ago in a far-away place. This biblical book contains truth which is beneficial for us today: "… and profitable for teaching, for reproof, for correction, for training in righteousness; so that the man of God may be adequate, equipped for every good work" (2 Tim. 3:16b–17). Because we are the people of God, 2 Samuel is our story. In this short commentary we will focus upon two particular ways in which 2 Samuel can benefit each of us.

First, everything recorded in Scripture points to God's

great work of redeeming His people through our Lord Jesus Christ, of whom it was said after His resurrection, "Then beginning with Moses and with all the prophets, He explained to them the things concerning Himself in all the Scriptures" (Luke 24:27). "He said to them, 'These are My words which I spoke to you while I was still with you, that all things which are written about Me in the Law of Moses and the Prophets and the Psalms must be fulfilled'" (Luke 24:44). The history recorded in the Scriptures is the unfolding of God's magnificent plan of redemption. While the stories of the Old Testament have moral applications, they are not merely moral. My objective is to show you Christ on every page of 2 Samuel. While there is much about David to be admired as a man after God's own heart and even a type of Christ, one of the great lessons of 2 Samuel is that the best king Israel ever produced was still a sinner who needed grace. The book of 2 Samuel shows us that we need a divine King, one far greater than David.

Second, the events recorded in 2 Samuel were designed by God to teach us how to live today. Paul, writing about the historical events of the Old Testament, says, "Now these things happened to them as an example, and they were written for our instruction, upon whom the ends of the ages have come" (1 Cor. 10:11). Jesus made moral application from an Old Testament event when he said, "Remember Lot's wife" (Luke 17:32). While biblical narratives typically record historical events without much comment or moral evaluation, these books are to be read through the lens of the teaching of the other sections of Scripture. These Old Testament stories powerfully illustrate the principles contained in God's Law and in the Wisdom Literature. For example, while Proverbs warns us about sexual temptation (Prov. 7), the tragic story of David's fall and its consequences paints a full-color picture of this truth (2 Sam. 11–12). As we work our way through 2 Samuel we will see the practical life lessons God has for us and we will be reproved, corrected, trained, and equipped for good works.

Finally, the objective in this commentary is not only to show both the redemptive focus and the practical application in 2 Samuel. My hope is that, as you go through 2 Samuel, you will learn to read all of Scripture, especially the historical narratives, in such a way that you will be able to find these truths for your own edification.

1 David is finally crowned as king of Israel

(1:1–5:25)

Imagine that it is Inauguration Day in the USA. After four years of his predecessor's failed policies, which have led the nation into economic crisis and foreign humiliation, a new President is being sworn in. The people are hopeful that a new day is dawning in America.

Then imagine that the popular new leader, in his first public speech as President, instead of criticizing his predecessor, praises him for his patriotism and for his attempts to lead the nation out of hard times. And then imagine that the new Head of State reads a poem which he has written in honor of the former President.

While such a scenario is unimaginable in modern politics, it reflects what David does after Saul's death. Even though Saul had repeatedly tried to assassinate him, David honors Saul in death and also treats those loyal to Saul, including his family members, with kindness and respect. This is even more amazing in light of the fact that in David's day, the first action of a new ruler was to eliminate the family and friends of the previous administration (as still happens in some parts of the world in our day). David conducts himself with dignity and grace because he trusts God to exalt him at the proper time.

David honors Saul and Jonathan in their deaths (1:1–27)

The book of 2 Samuel begins where 1 Samuel left off. The army of Israel has been defeated by the Philistines, with King Saul and his son and heir Jonathan being among the casualties. David, who had been on the run from Saul, was far from the battle. An Amalekite arrives in David's camp bringing what he thinks will be received as good news that David's enemy is dead (vv. 1–10). The Amalekite even claims to have, at Saul's request, performed what we would call a mercy killing upon the mortally wounded warrior (vv. 9–10). This messenger probably expected a reward from David,[1] but instead David puts him to death[2] for having the audacity to raise his hand against the king whom the LORD had anointed (vv. 14–16)—the very thing which David had repeatedly refused to do in 1 Samuel 24 and 26. Instead of rejoicing over the death of his enemy, David deeply mourns over the deaths of Saul and Jonathan (vv. 11–12). He sees their demise as a national tragedy for Israel.

David then composes a song of lament as an elegy for Saul and Jonathan (vv. 17–27). David calls upon his countrymen to honor the fallen king and his son as heroes of Israel. He remembers their deeds of valor. He is troubled that the Philistine idol-worshipers will celebrate their demise. In spite of the fact that Saul repeatedly sought to kill him, David does not rejoice over the downfall of his enemy.

David's determination not to take the kingdom by force, but to simply wait for the LORD to exalt him, is vindicated by Saul's death at the hands of the Philistines. David's exceptional character is further demonstrated as he continues to honor Saul, in spite of the evil that Saul had done against him. David shows that he will be a different kind of king.

David grows in strength (2:1–3:21)

After the deaths of Saul and Jonathan, David is the obvious choice to be the next king. Even so, he does not presume, but seeks guidance from the LORD before moving forward (2:1). The people of David's tribe of Judah anoint him as king (2:4a), while the other tribes, led by General Abner, place Saul's son, Ish-bosheth, on the throne of Israel (2:8–10). Again, David shows respect to his fallen enemy, Saul, by blessing the men of Jabesh-gilead who had given Saul a proper burial after the Philistines had put his body on shameful display (2:4b–7; 1 Sam. 31:11–13). This may also have been David's way of reaching out to the tribes of Israel in the hope of reuniting the kingdom.

Then a civil war erupts between Judah, led by David and General Joab, and Israel, led by Ish-bosheth and General Abner. Many die in battle, including Joab's brother Asahel (which will lead to a blood feud between the two generals). Over time, David's forces, led by Joab, prevail (2:17, 31; 3:1). The birth of sons also seems to indicate the strengthening of David's house (3:2–5).

General Abner, after a falling out with King Ish-bosheth,

promises to deliver the kingdom to David (3:6–12). David demands the return of his wife, Saul's daughter Michal (3:12–16). Abner makes good on his promise by persuading the elders of Israel to follow David (3:17–19), and then meets with David to seal the deal (3:20–21).

David is above reproach in the deaths of his enemies (3:22–4:13)

David's General Joab, after learning of Abner's successful machinations, murders Abner to avenge the death of his brother Asahel (3:22–30). Just as David had mourned over the death of Saul, so he now mourns over the death of his former enemy Abner, thus repudiating his assassination at the hands of Joab (3:28–29). David even composes another brief lament for the fallen general (3:31–39). David doesn't punish Joab at this time, because he is too strong (3:39).

One more man, Saul's son Ish-bosheth, stands between David having unchallenged authority in Israel. For a third time, David's enemy will be eliminated without David's hands being contaminated by the shedding of innocent blood. Two of former King Saul's commanders murder Ish-bosheth and bring his severed head to David in anticipation of a reward for their deed (4:1–8). David, rather than honoring the men who had assassinated his rival, executes them (4:9–12), just as he had done to the Amalekite who claimed to have killed King Saul.

David is very different from his predecessor Saul, who tried to murder David when he sensed him to be a potential rival. Rather than killing off his opponents or rejoicing over the deaths of his rivals, David shows himself to be a righteous ruler. The people take note of his being blameless in these sordid matters (3:36).

David is made king over all Israel (5:1–5)

Finally, after many years of running from Saul, courageously fighting the LORD's enemies, and waiting patiently, David is anointed king over all Israel. He is acknowledged as a man who will be a true shepherd to Israel (Ps. 78:70–72). He will enjoy a long reign.

David establishes his throne (5:6–25)

King David demonstrates his leadership and valor by dislodging the pagan Jebusites from Jerusalem, which will be his capital city (vv. 6–10). King Hiram of Tyre wisely honors David as king of Israel (vv. 11–12; Ps. 2:10–12). David's family continues to multiply (vv. 13–16). Then David decisively defeats Israel's great nemesis, the Philistines (vv. 17–25), thus bringing security and rest to the land.

After his years of trials and waiting, David can look back and say, "As the LORD lives, who has redeemed my life from all distress …" (4:9). Because the LORD God of hosts is with him, he is becoming greater and greater (5:10). His greatness is preserved as he continues to seek the LORD's guidance (v. 19) and as he gives God the glory for his success (v. 20). What could possibly go wrong?

Where do we see Jesus in this passage?

David showed himself to be a worthy leader of God's people. He was neither vengeful nor grasping. He was zealous for the LORD's honor. He sought and followed God's will. He was wise and patient as he endured suffering while awaiting his exaltation to the throne. Jesus surpasses David in each of these ways. Jesus is the true Anointed One who did not grasp at the kingdom when it was offered to Him through illegitimate means (Luke 4:1–13; John 6:15). Instead, He waited patiently through a time of suffering, refusing to avenge Himself against those who had wronged Him (1 Peter 2:21). Finally, at the perfect time, the Father exalted Him.

Just as David was gracious toward his enemies, so Jesus is most gracious to his enemies, resulting in our reconciliation to God (Rom. 5:10; Col. 1:21).

Just as David was called to shepherd Israel (5:2), so Jesus is the Good Shepherd who willingly laid down His life for His sheep (John 10:11–18).

If David could compose a song to sing the praises of a man like Saul (1:17–27), how much more ought we to sing the praises of our perfect and glorious King Jesus, who has conquered sin, Satan, and death on our behalf (Heb. 2:14–15)! The love of Christ is better than romantic love (1:26). He is our true Friend who has shown us the greatest possible love by giving His life for our benefit (John 15:13; 1 John 4:10). His love is most beautiful and pleasant (S. of S. 5:10; Isa. 4:2).

> If David could compose a song to sing the praises of a man like Saul, how much more ought we to sing the praises of our perfect and glorious King Jesus!

Just as Hiram acknowledged King David (5:11), so one day all rulers will acknowledge King Jesus (Ps. 2:10–12; Isa. 60:3).

How does this passage apply to us?

Rather than trying to advance yourself, trust God to exalt you when He sees fit. David's piety was greater than his ambition. Even though he had been anointed as the future king (1 Sam. 16:13), he waited for God to exalt him at the proper time. May God help us to be people who put His interests above self-interest, trusting Him to give us what is best in His time and way. We have a glorious destiny with Christ, but we may have to suffer patiently according to the will of God until the time of fulfillment (Ps. 52:8–9; Rom. 8:18).

David exemplified the biblical teaching "Never take your own revenge, beloved, but leave room for the wrath of God …" (Rom. 12:19). He refused to take revenge on Saul, and finally God's wrath came upon his enemy. Just as David was mistreated by Saul, so we are sometimes wounded by those who wrongfully harm us. How good it is to trust in God's justice so that we don't need to get even with those who treat us as enemies.

The scenario described by the Amalekite in which Saul allegedly begged to be put out of his misery (1:9–10) seems to fit what many would call a "mercy killing," but David judged this Amalekite guilty because he was not authorized to take life. We are not authorized by God to participate in "euthanasia," even if the person who is dying begs us to do so. Though there is nothing wrong with giving those who suffer strong medications to relieve their pain (Prov. 31:6–7), only God is authorized to take life (1 Sam. 2:6; Deut. 32:39; Exod. 20:13).

Some modern scholars have twisted David's statement

of love for Jonathan in 1:26, especially the phrase "Your love to me was more wonderful than the love of women," to make it seem as if David and Jonathan were involved in a homosexual relationship. Such an interpretation is more a reflection of the modern impulse to justify homosexuality than an honest attempt to exegete the text of Scripture. Men can have deep non-sexual friendships which are honoring to the Lord. David and Jonathan encouraged one another spiritually. A relationship which violates God's law would have been destructive to their souls (Lev. 18:22; 20:13). The love of David and Jonathan was not sexual, but one of faithful friendship (Prov. 18:24; 17:17) in which each was willing to make great sacrifices for the good of the other (1 Sam. 18:1–4; 20:1–42; 23:16–18). The reference to the love of women is used to contrast romantic/sexual love with the friendship they enjoyed.[3]

We can follow David's example of seeking God's guidance, though we get direction not from seers, but through His all-sufficient Word (2 Tim. 3:16–17). We can also follow David in giving glory to the LORD for all our victories (5:19–20).

The seeds of future destruction can be sown during times of blessing. David multiplied wives for himself (2:2; 3:2–5, 12–16; 5:13–16). God had given Adam but one wife, and through Moses had warned rulers against having more than one wife (Deut. 17:17). David's inordinate desire for women would prove to be his ruin. The mention of David's many sons also foreshadows the tragic events recorded in the latter part of 2 Samuel.

FOR FURTHER STUDY

1. Did the Amalekite really kill Saul? Or was he making up a story in hopes of getting a reward (1:6–10; 1 Sam. 31:5–6)?

2. Why, in light of the fact that he already had several other wives, was David so insistent that Michal be returned to him (3:13–16)?

3. Why didn't David punish Joab for murdering Abner, especially in light of the fact that he executed the Amalekite who killed Saul and the murderers of Ish-bosheth (3:39; also see 1 Kings 2:5–6, 28–35)?

4. How did David's hardships prepare him to be a good king?

5. How is Jesus fully qualified to be our King (Deut. 17:14–20; Ezek. 34:23; 37:24)?

6. If the people of Israel knew that the LORD had anointed David to shepherd Israel (5:2), why did they wait so long to acknowledge him?

7. How does David's call to shepherd Israel relate to the call of pastors to shepherd the church (5:2; 1 Peter 5:1–5; Acts 20:28)?

8. What was the justification for David's attack upon the Jebusites in Jerusalem (5:6–9; Ps. 139:19–22)?

9. Why did David make Jerusalem his capital?

TO THINK ABOUT AND DISCUSS

1. Is it ever justified and merciful to help someone to die (1:9–10)?

2. How would you answer someone who claimed, on the basis of 1:26, that David and Jonathan had a homosexual relationship?

3. How did David portray the qualities of an ideal ruler (Prov. 20:8, 26; 25:5)?

4. What do we learn from David about what we should expect of our political and religious leaders?

5. Are there times when practical considerations prevent us from acting justly (3:39)?

6. How does God guide our decisions (5:19)?

7. In light of David's rejection of those who promoted his kingdom by unjust means, how should Christians view the Crusades?

8. In what kind of warfare are we engaged (Eph. 6:12; 2 Cor. 10:3–6)?

2 The danger and joy of drawing near to a holy God

(6:1–23)

We live in a day in which many people are very casual about the things of God. Religious pluralists claim that any effort to worship God is a good thing so long as people are sincere.

Even professing evangelicals are very lax in their approach to worship, often disregarding biblical teaching about how the Lord wants us to approach Him. In this chapter, we see how critical it is that we approach our holy God according to the ways he has prescribed.

The desire for God's presence: David seeks to move the ark to Jerusalem (vv. 1–2)

David's life has been on the upswing. His domestic and foreign enemies have been vanquished. He has been making all the right moves as king and has the love and respect of the people. David, as a man after God's own heart (Acts 13:22), is a king who is devoted to worship. He composed numerous psalms of praise which are still central in our worship today. It is because of his passionate heart for God that he wants to bring the ark of God to his capital city of Jerusalem. Later David will further express his devotion to the LORD by seeking to build a temple in Jerusalem (7:1–2).

The ark of God was a gold-plated wooden box just under four feet long and just over two feet wide and tall. It contained a jar holding manna, Aaron's rod which had budded, and the stone tablets of the Ten Commandments (Exod. 25:10–22; Heb. 9:4). On top of the ark was the mercy seat, the place of propitiatory sacrifice which served as a reminder that God's people can be reconciled to Him only through blood sacrifice (Lev. 16:14–15). The mercy seat was guarded by golden cherubim, a symbol of the fact that access to God's holy presence is restricted. The ark was equipped with gold rings so that it could be carried by the Levites using poles. The ark was most holy because it represented the LORD's presence among His people (Exod. 25:22).

The ark of God played an important role in 1 Samuel. The Israelites tried to bring it into battle, only to have it taken by the Philistines who, after much suffering, returned it. The awesomeness of the ark was further demonstrated when many in Israel died after failing to respect its holiness (1 Sam. 6:19). Since then, other than one incident when Saul took the ark into battle (1 Sam. 14:18), the ark seems to have rested in obscurity and disuse.

David's desire to bring the ark to Jerusalem is good. He wants to restore proper worship to Israel so that the people of God can draw near to Him. He wants to give the ark, which represents the LORD's presence, a place of prominence in Israel so that the LORD Himself will be exalted as He reigns over His people. David plans a great procession with a grand celebration.

The failed pursuit of God's presence: David learns about the LORD's holiness (vv. 3–11)

When it comes to seeking God's presence, however, good intentions are not enough. David arranges for the ark of God to be placed on a new cart and for it to be moved to Jerusalem under the supervision of Uzzah and Ahio (vv. 3–4). David joins the procession with great celebration (v. 5). It seems that this day will be the culmination of centuries of hope. Israel has a great king who is bringing the ark into his holy city. The instruments are playing and the people are rejoicing.

Then disaster strikes. The oxen pulling the cart stumble, and as the ark appears to be falling to the ground, Uzzah reaches out his hand to steady it (v. 6). Immediately he is struck dead (v. 7). The celebration is over. The occasion of great joy has suddenly become a time of overwhelming sorrow.[1]

Many might think that the LORD acted in a way which was harsh, arbitrary, or unfair. The problem is not, however, with God, but with us. He is infinitely holy. He had specifically revealed how the ark was to be transported: by certain men (the descendants of Kohath) from among the Levites and using poles (Deut. 10:8; Num. 4:4–10). The (unauthorized) idea of using the cart seems to have come from the Philistines (1 Sam. 6:7). The LORD had also made it very clear that no one was to look into or even touch His ark (Num. 4:15; 1 Sam. 6:19). Uzzah treated the ark as if it was common, not holy. He arrogantly presumed that his sinful hands were cleaner than dirt. He, along with David and all Israel, failed to show proper reverence for the LORD's holiness. God is glorious, a consuming fire (Deut. 4:24; Heb. 12:29). Instead of complaining of the LORD's harshness, we should marvel at His mercy in that only Uzzah died, instead of the whole company including David.

David responds with a variety of emotions. First he is angry (v. 8). Then he becomes fearful and discouraged (vv. 9–20). Finally he becomes hopeful again, as he sees that God wants to bless His people as they draw near to Him in the right way (vv. 11–12). In the past, David had inquired of the LORD before making major decisions (5:19), but this time he had acted without even considering what God had already revealed in His Word.

The joy of drawing near to a holy God (vv. 12–19)

After the death of Uzzah, the ark of the LORD remained in the house of Obed-edom for three months. When Obed-edom's house was blessed, David realized that the problem was not with the ark, but with Israel's misuse of the ark. First Chronicles 15:11–15 records David's repentance for having failed to follow the LORD's Word the first time he moved the ark, and his determination carefully to follow the Scriptures this time. King David leads God's people in joyful procession as the ark of the LORD enters Jerusalem. The people sing and shout as various musical instruments are played (v. 15; 1 Chr. 15:27–28). As the ark is put in a place of prominence in the tent of meeting, David offers sacrifices before the LORD (through the Aaronic priests). Finally, he blesses the people and gives them a generous gift of food as they return to their homes.

This has been a historic day in the life of Israel. The ark of the LORD has found a resting place in the holy city of Jerusalem. David shows himself to be a worthy king who leads the people to passionately serve and obey the LORD.

David's divided household(vv. 16, 20–23)

Not everyone is impressed with King David's enthusiasm for the LORD, however. One of his wives, Michal, who is also a daughter of former King Saul, looks upon David's zeal with contempt (v. 16). When David returns home to bless his family, she accuses him of having acted shamelessly (v. 20). This is the first of many problems King David will have with his family. David forcefully defends his devotion to the LORD and contrasts it with the unfaithfulness of Michal's father, Saul. Michal's scorn will not stop David from humbly and joyfully worshiping the LORD (Isa. 57:10). The author records that Michal remained childless (a tragedy for a woman in that day) as a consequence of her ungodliness and a vindication of David's zeal for the LORD (v. 23). This also meant that there would be no merging of the royal lines of Saul and David. Michal would not bear the prince who would be king. Nor would she be included in the Messianic line.

Where do we see Jesus in this passage?

In the 1981 movie *Raiders of the Lost Ark,* Indiana Jones and others search for the lost ark of God. We have good news. We have found Him. Jesus fulfills what the ark represents and replaces it as the place where God meets His people. Through Him, God is present with us. His name is Immanuel, which means "God with us" (Isa. 7:14; Matt. 1:23). He is holy (Luke 1:35; 4:34; Acts 2:27). He reveals God to us (John 1:1, 14; Col. 2:9).

It is through Jesus that we are able to draw near to God. We are as unclean and unfit for God's presence as Uzzah was. Jesus, however, stood in our place and received the punishment we deserved (Isa. 53:10). What happened to Uzzah happened to Jesus, who died under God's wrath. His death is even more shocking than that of Uzzah, because Jesus was innocent. Jesus was struck down on the cross because He bore *our* guilt (2 Cor. 5:21). Through His work we are reconciled to God (Rom. 3:25; 1 John 2:2). Through Him we can now safely draw near to God (John 14:6; Heb. 10:19–23).

However, if anyone tries to enter God's presence in any way other than through Jesus, he or she will, like Uzzah, perish (John 14:6; Acts 4:12). This means that every other form of religion, no matter how sincerely followed, leads to death. Mankind continues to build "carts" like those of the Philistines, and, like Uzzah, to underestimate the pollution of our sin. We must approach God in the only way He has prescribed. Even those who claim to be Christians but believe that they can, through their own good works and religious acts, contribute to their salvation are as unfit as Uzzah for the presence of God. They remain under God's wrath until they trust solely in Christ for their salvation.

One day you, like Uzzah, will stand in the presence of our holy God. Do you acknowledge that you, like Uzzah, are unclean and that God is infinitely holy? Do you trust in the work of Jesus alone to give you the holiness you lack so that you can safely draw near to God by faith? None but Jesus can do helpless sinners good.

The glorious scene of David entering Jerusalem with the ark of God is a picture of the coming of the Messiah to reign over His people. The Psalms portray the LORD Himself entering His holy city (Ps. 24). Jesus is the King who, more than David, is worthy to ascend the hill of the LORD because He has clean hands and a pure heart (Ps. 24:3–4). Jesus leads us in joyful procession into God's holy presence, having removed our filth by His sacrifice for us (Heb. 9:28). Just as David gave up his royal robes for a linen ephod (6:14), so Jesus clothed Himself as a servant and gladly associates with the lowly (Phil. 2:5–8; John 13:1–17; Matt. 20:28). Just as David fed his people and gave them gifts on the day of celebration (6:19), so Jesus feeds His people and distributes gifts to them (John 6:47–51; Eph. 4:8). Just as David triumphantly entered Jerusalem with the ark of God, so Jesus triumphantly entered Jerusalem in His first coming (Luke 19:28–44), and on the last day He will enter His holy city to reign forever (Ps. 24:7–10; Rev. 21:1–5).

Like David, Jesus is zealous for God's honor (John 2:17; Ps. 69:9). And, like David, Jesus is rejected by those who are of the flesh, even his own family (6:16, 20; John 1:11; 7:5).

How does this passage apply to us?

The LORD is still holy and is not to be trifled with. Those who fail to respect His holiness will, like Uzzah, come under His judgment. That which is directly connected to God is to be treated with reverence. God's name is holy and is not to be taken in vain (Exod. 20:7). Those who misuse his name or use it as a curse will one day incur His wrath. God's Word is holy. Those who treat the Bible as merely a human book and stand in judgment over it as critics or dare to add or subtract from Holy Scripture are inviting judgment upon themselves (Rev. 22:18–19; Deut. 18:19). God's church is His holy dwelling place in this age (Eph. 2:21–22; 1 Peter 2:5). He has told us how to run His church (1 Tim. 3:15), including instructing us on the role of women (1 Tim. 2:9–15) and the qualifications of church leaders (1 Tim. 3:1–13). We are not free to turn from His ways to worldly ways when it comes to managing Christ's church.

> We are not free to turn from God's ways to worldly ways when it comes to managing Christ's church.

God's worship is most holy. Just as Uzzah was struck dead, so Nadab and Abihu were consumed by fire which came out from the presence of the LORD when they offered unauthorized worship before Him (Lev. 10:1–2). Such judgments also occur under the New Covenant. Some who didn't properly regard the Lord's Supper became ill and others died (1 Cor. 11:27–32). Ananias and his wife Sapphira were struck dead when they lied about the money they gave to the Lord's work (Acts 5:1–11). God has set aside the Lord's Day as a holy day in which we are to make a priority of gathering with His people (Heb. 10:25) to worship Him in spirit and in truth (John 4:24). Just as Israel was not free to replace what God had prescribed about moving the ark with their own ideas, so we are not free to replace what God has prescribed in Scripture with our own ideas. Jesus warned the Jews of His day, "You invalidated the word of God for the sake of your tradition" (Matt. 15:6). Some churches have added altars, incense, statues, human mediators, and extra-biblical sacraments to the worship of God. Others have shaped their worship to fit the surrounding culture, just as the Israelites followed the Philistines in using a cart to carry the ark of God. What is supposed to be God-centered worship becomes man-centered entertainment aimed at making visitors feel comfortable. Preaching is replaced with a dramatic presentation or a film. Music is chosen for the purpose of appealing to the target audience. Such "worship" simply affirms people's belief that they, as religious consumers, are the center of the universe, rather than challenging them with the fact that God is. The worship of the Old Testament, including the use of the ark of God, was not designed to please or entertain men and women. Rather it was to reflect the awesome glory of God. In the same way, New Testament worship is to be God-centered and is regulated by Scripture, not human whims.

Worship is the work of acknowledging the greatness of God (Ps. 95:6; 96:8–9). All people owe God worship (Rom. 1:20–21; Matt. 4:10), but most do not truly honor Him. We have been saved that we might worship God (1 Peter 2:5, 9). He calls His people to worship Him corporately as we offer Him a sacrifice of praise (Heb. 10:25; 13:15–16).

Our worship is to be Christ-centered as we draw near to God through Jesus (John 14:6; Heb. 10:19–22). He is our King who leads us into God's holy presence, having made a way for us to enter the holiest place through His blood. Our redemption in Christ is the focal point in our worship as we emphasize not what we can do for Him, but what He has done for us.

While worship under the New Covenant is significantly different from Old Covenant worship (John 4:21–23; Gal. 4:9–11), God is still holy and must only be approached in the way He has revealed (Heb. 12:28–29). Just as God prescribed rules for the worship of Israel, so we are called to worship Him according to His revealed truth (John 4:24; Acts 2:42). These elements include the reading and proclamation of God's Word (2 Tim. 4:1–4; 1 Tim. 4:13), prayer (1 Tim. 2:1–8; Acts 1:14; 13:3; 4:24–31; Rev. 5:8), the singing of God's praises (Eph. 5:18–20; Col. 3:15–16), and the Lord's Supper (Acts 2:42; 20:7; 1 Cor. 11:23–26). While there are circumstances of worship (such as the time we meet on the Lord's day, the style of music, a common cup or many cups in communion, etc.) in which we have freedom, we are not free to add to or to subtract from the elements of worship revealed in the New Testament. By giving time to unbiblical worship we take away precious time which should be given to the worship which God seeks, and worshipers may be subjected to elements of worship that would go against their consciences. Nor are we free to go back to Old Covenant worship, because its types and shadows have been fulfilled in Christ (1 Tim. 2:5; Heb. 8:13; Col. 2:23). We need to be vigilant because human nature seems very prone to replacing God's Word with human traditions (Matt. 15:3).

When David successfully drew near to God in worship, he not only worshiped according to truth, he also was full of holy enthusiasm—worshiping in spirit (John 4:24). It is not enough to get worship right in its external elements. We must also worship the Lord from the heart. There are two kinds of danger when it comes to emotions in worship. Some indulge in careless enthusiasm in which they seek an emotional experience which is self-centered and may not even be connected with divine truth. The other extreme is that some of us might, like David's wife Michal (6:16), be uncomfortable or even judgmental about anyone who worships God with great emotion. Worship is the highest and most joyful human activity. The truths of God's Word, especially redemption, should stir our emotions. David was thrilled at God's goodness and was not concerned about what others thought of him (6:20–22; Prov. 29:25). We should be wholehearted in our worship, even if we aren't great singers or eloquent in prayer. Worship is enhanced when we stop thinking about ourselves and become consumed with making much of God. It is ironic that people who have no problem expressing their emotional enthusiasm at a sporting event or a political rally feel that they need to be exceptionally reserved in worship. On the other hand, we should not, like Michal (6:20), judge others for how outwardly expressive their worship is. What matters is the heart. "Bless the LORD, O my soul, and all that is within me, bless His holy name" (Ps. 103:1).

The conflict between David and his wife Michal is a reminder of how important it is to marry someone who is

> Worship is enhanced when we stop thinking about ourselves and become consumed with making much of God.

spiritually compatible (2 Cor. 6:14–18; 1 Cor. 7:39; 9:5). An ungodly spouse will tear you down with his or her words (Eph. 4:29; Prov. 12:18) and will tear down your home (Prov. 14:1). David appears to have been initially attracted to Michal for the wrong reasons, including her status as the daughter of a king (1 Sam. 18:20–29). A potential mate can be physically attractive and have charm and class, but if he or she doesn't fear God, you are in for a hard marriage (Prov. 31:30). By contrast, a spouse who loves the LORD will build you up and draw you closer to the LORD (Prov. 18:22; Eph. 5:25–27).

David's experience with Michal also reminds us that following Christ will put us at odds with those who are of the world (John 18:36; 15:18–20; 17:14). As the world becomes more corrupt and godless we will find ourselves experiencing contempt and even persecution in our schools, workplaces, neighborhoods, and even our families. Jesus warned that our family members, including our parents and our children, may despise us because we follow Christ (Matt. 10:34–36). Those who are in the darkness hate the light (John 3:19). They think that we are fools (1 Cor. 1:18; 2:14). We, like David, must overcome the fear of man as we are controlled, not by what people think, but by our devotion to Christ (Prov. 29:25; Luke 14:26–27). One day we, like David, will be vindicated (Mark 10:29–31).

For further study ▶

FOR FURTHER STUDY

1. Why did the LORD establish detailed rules concerning the treatment of the ark of God?

2. Why was Uzzah's death just?

3. Why don't we possess the ark of God today? What would the significance be if it were to be found? Were the people who made the movie *Raiders of the Lost Ark* right about its power?

4. How is the scene of David entering Jerusalem with the ark of God a picture of the coming of Christ?

5. In what ways is New Testament worship different from Old Testament worship? Are there any similarities?

6. Why did Michal despise David?

7. David fought hard to gain Michal as his wife (1 Sam. 18:20–29) and went to great efforts to get her back when he was made king (2 Sam. 3:13–16). Why was she so important to him? Was she worth it?

TO THINK ABOUT AND DISCUSS.

1. How should our leaders show their passion for the Lord (6:5)?

2. How would you answer someone who said that God's wrath is harsh and unfair (6:7)?

3. Are you tempted to be angry when your plans don't work out? How is such anger ultimately anger toward God (6:8; James 4:13–17)?

4. Our pluralistic "tolerant" culture is offended by the truths taught in this passage—that God is holy and that He will punish those who lack the holiness He requires. How can we faithfully present these truths to a hostile culture?

5. Make a list of the elements of worship taught in the New Testament.

6. Can it ever be justified to leave any biblical element out of our worship services, even for one week?

7. What are the unbiblical elements some add to Christian worship in our day? What harm is caused by these?

8. Make a list of the aspects of worship in which we have freedom.

9. What place should emotions have in our worship? Are there ways in which you need to grow in expressing your emotions in corporate worship?

10. Why do unbelievers, including family members, look down upon those who passionately serve and worship God?

11. What can we learn from David's marriage to Michal about the importance of choosing a godly spouse and the troubles which can come through marriage to an unbeliever?

3 The LORD builds a house for David

(7:1–29)

We have come to one of the most important passages, not just in 2 Samuel, but in the entire Bible. David is at the pinnacle of his power. He is king over all Israel. His enemies are subdued. He desires to build a house for God in Jerusalem.

The LORD responds by saying that, instead, it is He who will build a house for David. We call the LORD's declaration the Davidic covenant. It is the unconditional promise of an ongoing dynasty for David which will culminate in the everlasting reign of the Messiah. This promise becomes a reference point for the rest of Scripture and the basis of Israel's hope during hard times of oppression and exile.

David wants to do something great for the LORD (vv. 1–3)

David is enjoying a season of prosperity and security. After years of being chased as a fugitive and hiding in caves, he is firmly established as the king over all Israel and is living in his palace in his capital city of Jerusalem. The rest that he and the nation enjoy is the fulfillment of the covenant hope of Israel (Deut. 12:10; 25:19). If you have read through this history of Israel during the times of the judges and King Saul, you will realize that such peace and security is a rare and precious thing.

In the midst of all this prosperity, David desires to build a house (temple) as a dwelling place of God (through His ark) among His people. The Law spoke of the day when God's people would have rest and security so that a permanent place for worship would be established (Deut. 12:10–12). David's desire is commendable. Rather than using his wealth to increase the greatness of his own name, he seeks the glory of God (Ps. 132:4–5). He acknowledges that the LORD is the author of his success and he wants to express his gratitude (5:12; Ps. 116:12).

David wisely seeks counsel from the prophet Nathan, whose initial response is very positive (v. 3). Later, Nathan receives revelation from God telling David not to build the house (vv. 4–7). How could God's prophet be wrong? While it is true that prophecy is infallible, prophets, when not speaking under the inspiration of God, are fallible (see also 1 Sam. 1:14; 16:6–7). Nathan's initial answer was simply his assessment of the situation based upon the worthiness of David's desire.

The LORD is going to do something great for David (vv. 4–17)

David's human plan (dream) is corrected by divine revelation. The Word of the LORD comes to the prophet Nathan in one of the longest (197 words) and most significant monologues from the LORD since the days of Moses. These words establish the Davidic covenant which becomes Israel's hope for the next thousand years.

David is not the one who will build a house for the LORD (vv. 5–7). The LORD has no complaint about not having a house in Israel. No physical building can contain Him (1 Kings 8:27; Isa. 66:1). Elsewhere, David reveals that he was not chosen to build a house for the LORD because he was a man of bloodshed in all his wars (1 Chr. 22:6–8). Instead, David's son Solomon, who would be a man of rest and peace, would have the privilege of building the temple (1 Chr. 22:9–10). David would, however, make extensive preparations for the building of this temple (1 Chr. 22:14–19).

> The LORD reveals that instead of David doing great things for the LORD, the LORD will do great things for David.

The LORD reveals that instead of David doing great things for the LORD, the LORD will do great things for David. He has chosen David to be ruler over His people Israel and He is making David's name great (vv. 8–9). This is an echo of the LORD's promise to make Abraham great (Gen. 12:2), thereby putting His covenant promise to David alongside the foundational covenant with Abraham. The name of David will be among those of the great men who have lived on the earth.

The LORD also promises to continue to do great things for David in the future. Israel will be securely planted in the Promised Land, where they will enjoy prosperity and rest

(vv. 10–11a). There is a significant play on words. Instead of David building a literal *house* for the LORD (v. 5), the LORD will build an everlasting *house* (dynasty) for David (v. 11b). Unlike Saul, whose dynasty ended with his death (v. 15), David will have a descendant who will reign in his place and will build a house (temple) for the LORD (vv. 12–13a). David is promised a dynasty that will endure forever (vv. 13b, 15–16).

David expresses praise and gratitude to the LORD (vv. 18–29)

David responds in prayer to the LORD's covenant promise to build his house. Rather than being disappointed that his original plan to build a house for the LORD has been rejected, David is full of thanks for all the great things that God has done and will do for him (vv. 18–20). David also acknowledges the uniqueness of God (vv. 21–22; Isa. 45:5–7) and the greatness of His redeeming works for His people (vv. 23–24). Finally, David asks the LORD to do just as He has promised, by blessing the house of David forever (vv. 25–29).

When and how were the covenant promises to David fulfilled?

Some promises were fulfilled in David's lifetime, as David was made ruler over all Israel, his enemies were defeated, he gained a great name as Israel was established as a world power, and the LORD gave Israel security and rest in the land (vv. 8–11). The promises that David would have a son to reign after him and who would build a house for the LORD were fulfilled in Solomon (vv. 12–13a; 1 Kings 8:20). Other promises were fulfilled in David's ongoing dynasty as the LORD took a special interest in David's descendants, disciplining them (including Solomon) when they sinned, but not allowing David's house to perish (vv. 13b–15; Ps. 89:33–37). First and Second Kings record God's faithfulness to His covenant with David as David's sons reigned in Judah for over four hundred years. Even when their sin became intolerable and the kingdom was taken away, the LORD preserved the line of David (Matt. 1:12–17). During the dark days of Israel's exile and oppression under foreign dominion, the LORD's covenant promise to David sustained the faithful (Ps. 89; Isa. 9:6–7; Jer. 23:5–6; Zech. 12:7–8; Ezek. 34:23–24). From what appeared to be the dead stump of David's posterity, new life would appear.

> Then a shoot will spring from the stem of Jesse, and a branch from his roots will bear fruit. The Spirit of the LORD will rest on Him. Isaiah 11:1–2

> In that day I will raise up the fallen booth of David, and wall up its breaches; I will also raise up its ruins and rebuild it as in the days of old. Amos 9:11

> My servant David will be king over them, and they will all have one shepherd; and they will walk in My ordinances and keep My statutes and observe them. They will live on the land that I gave to Jacob My servant, in which your fathers lived; and they will live on it, they, and their sons and their sons' sons, forever; and David My servant will be their prince forever. Ezekiel 37:24–25

Where do we see Jesus in this passage?

Jesus Christ is the ultimate fulfillment of God's promises

to David. There was an immediate fulfillment of God's promises to David through his son Solomon and the other Davidic kings who followed. But none of these kings fulfilled God's promise that a son of David would reign over Israel forever (vv. 13, 16; Ps. 89:28–29). Furthermore, Solomon and his successors all fell short of the righteousness God required of the true king of Israel. All the LORD's wonderful promises to David pointed to David's greater son, Jesus (Heb. 1:5; Isa. 9:7; Ps. 89:26–27). Jesus appeared at just the right time, in a very dark day in Israel when only a remnant clung to hope (John 7:42). He was the true Seed of David, the Son of God, who reigns on David's throne (vv. 12, 14a, 16). "He will be great and will be called the Son of the Most High; and the Lord God will give Him the throne of His father David; and He will reign over the house of Jacob forever, and His kingdom will have no end" (Luke 1:32–33; see also Heb. 1:5; Rom. 1:3). Jesus was chastised, not for his own iniquities, but for ours (7:14b; Isa. 53:4–5; Heb. 5:8–9). Jesus is the Son of David who lives and reigns forever (Heb. 1:8). The grave itself could not hold Him (Acts 2:30–31; 13:34). Jesus builds a house (temple) for God's dwelling, the church (Matt. 16:18; 1 Peter 2:5; Eph. 2:19; Rev. 21:22). In Jesus we have everlasting rest (2 Sam. 7:13; Isa. 53:10; Heb. 4:9–11). Jesus is the fulfillment of the Davidic covenant in answer to David's prayers (7:25–29).

How does this passage apply to us?

How well do you handle prosperity? Times of blessing can be dangerous (Prov. 30:8–9). Jesus taught that "It is easier for a camel to go through the eye of a needle, than for a rich man to enter the kingdom of God" (Matt. 19:24). Part of what makes David remarkable is that he recognized that his success was from God and he wanted to honor the LORD as an expression of his gratitude (vv. 1–2). We have been blessed with every spiritual blessing in Christ. Many of us are also blessed materially. Will we build bigger barns to store our wealth, or will we be rich toward God (Luke 12:18–21)?

Do you, like David, seek wise counsel when you are making important decisions (vv. 2–3; Prov. 12:15; 13:10)? When you are counseling others, do you diligently seek guidance from God's Word, which is your only authority, before giving an answer? Nathan appears to have spoken too quickly (vv. 3–7). Counselors must be careful to distinguish between when they are speaking on the authority of God's Word and when they are giving a fallible personal opinion. For example, we can say from Scripture that a single Christian should marry only another believer (1 Cor. 9:5; 7:39). On the other hand, we may have an opinion about which believer he or she should marry, but our opinion is not authoritative.

Just as David's worthy dream of personally building a house for God in his lifetime was not fulfilled because it was not God's will, so we may have dreams which turn out not to be part of God's plan for our lives (James 4:13–17). Some of our unfulfilled dreams may reflect a great desire to honor God by being a missionary, planting a church, establishing a new ministry, or beginning a new family. Even our very strong desires which may be motivated by good intentions may not necessarily be God's will. We have to trust that God's will is best (Rom. 8:28). God may have called you to be like David, who did the hard work which laid the basis for his successor Solomon to build the temple.

Second Samuel 7 points us to the gospel. Many people view religion as what we do for God. Like the ancient kings who would build temples to their gods and offer sacrifices, today people of various religions try to gain God's favor by their good works and religious ceremonies. The message of the gospel, however, is that we trust not in what we do for God, but in what He has done for us through Jesus Christ. Salvation is His work and not ours (1 Cor. 1:30–31). We are saved by grace, through faith, apart from works, and even our faith itself is a gift of God (Eph. 2:8–9). Becoming a Christian involves giving up on trying to earn God's favor by doing something great for Him, and instead relying solely upon the great work He has done for us through the cross of Jesus Christ. Then, as those who have been saved solely by God's work, we offer Him our worship and our service, not to earn His favor, but out of love and gratitude. We also learn that when we give to Him, He gives us back far more

God's covenant promises to David are ours in Christ (Gal. 3:14, 26–29). We who were once excluded from the covenants are adopted sons and heirs (Eph. 2:11, 19; Acts 15:14–18; Gal.

> God's covenant promises to David are ours in Christ.

4:7; Rom. 8:18). One day we will reign with Christ in His everlasting kingdom (2 Tim. 2:12; Rev. 3:21). The security of our standing is not based upon our faithfulness, but upon the covenant faithfulness of the LORD. Because God loves us as sons, He will discipline us when we stray (2 Sam. 7:14b; Prov.

3:11–12; Heb. 12:4–11). We, like David, should joyfully praise God as we marvel at His gracious choice of us and as we await the certain and final fulfillment of all His promises to us (7:18–29). Just as the LORD worked a great redemption for Israel, so He has done great things in redeeming us (7:23–24; 1 Peter 1:18–19; 2:9–10).

FOR FURTHER STUDY

1. Why is 2 Samuel 7 one of the most important chapters in the Bible?

2. How does Jesus fulfill the Old Covenant hope of rest in the land?

3. Contrast David's response to prosperity with that of Babylonian King Nebuchadnezzar (Dan. 4:29–30).

4. How could Nathan the prophet be wrong about David's plan (7:3; see also 1 Sam. 1:14; 16:6–7)?

5. Why was God's sovereignty over all things a necessary condition for the fulfillment of His covenant promises in the distant future (7:19)?

6. How did the promises of the Davidic covenant point to Christ?

TO THINK ABOUT AND DISCUSS

1. What are your dreams and desires for serving God?

2. How can you know if your plans and dreams are according to God's will?

3. Which is more important: what we do for God, or what God does for us? Explain your answer.

4. How should God's faithfulness to His covenant promises motivate our faithfulness to our promises (e.g. marriage—Ps. 15:4; Matt. 19:6)?

5. How does the Davidic covenant have evangelistic value (Acts 13:23; 2:30)?

6. How does 7:22 address the religious pluralism which is popular in our day?

7. Why did David need to pray for what the LORD had already promised to do (7:25–29; see also Dan. 9:15–19)? How do God's promises fuel our prayers?

8. How can you use David's prayer as a model prayer in your own life?

4 David's triumphs and his lovingkindness

(8:1–10:19)

This section of 2 Samuel shows David at his very best. He crushes his enemies and brings further peace and prosperity to Israel. He is an able administrator. He also shows himself to be a man of integrity and compassion. Sadly, these chapters also mark the high point of King David's reign. After this, David will be guilty of a disastrous moral failure which will result in many hardships.

David triumphs over Israel's enemies (8:1–18)

King David defeats his foes in every direction, subduing the Philistines to the west (v. 1), smiting Moab to the east (v. 2), and conquering others to the north and south (vv. 3–6, 13–14). David also enriches himself and Israel with the spoils of war from those he defeats (vv. 4, 7–8) and receives tribute from neighboring kingdoms (vv. 2b, 9–10). In addition, David wisely and righteously administers his kingdom by establishing civil justice and by delegating authority to trusted subordinates (vv. 15–18).

Some readers will be troubled by David's aggressive foreign policy, including the slaughter of his foes (v. 2a). But David is engaging in holy war on the LORD's behalf, bringing righteous judgment upon wicked idolaters who rejected the LORD and His anointed one (Deut. 7:1–6, 23–26; Ps. 2:10–12). David faithfully carries out God's Law concerning the surrounding nations (Deut. 20). David's success is credited to the LORD: "And the LORD helped David wherever he went" (vv. 6b, 14b; see also Ps. 20:7). The establishment of David's great name is in fulfillment of God's covenant promises to David (7:9–11; 8:13). The capture of the land fulfills God's promises to Abraham (Gen. 15:18), Moses (Deut. 11:24), and Joshua (Josh. 1:4). David is an ideal king who reflects God's righteous rule and leads his people into a golden age of rest. For centuries, Jews would look back on David's reign with fondness. But, thankfully, David's kingdom was not the final fulfillment of God's promise.

David shows lovingkindness to Mephibosheth (9:1–13)

This is one of the sweetest stories in the Bible and would probably be more popular among preachers if the main character's name wasn't so hard to pronounce. David has already shown himself to be an ideal king by his valor in battle and by honoring the LORD in his victories. Now he shows his greatness by acting with lovingkindness toward a man whom other kings of his era would have killed.

As David is enjoying such great success he decides to show kindness to someone from the house of his predecessor, King

Saul, for the sake of Saul's son, Jonathan, with whom David had made a covenant (v. 1; 1 Sam. 20:8). Many years earlier, when David was a fugitive whom Saul was seeking to kill, Jonathan had shown kindness to David at great personal risk. David swore that when he became king, he would treat Jonathan's family with similar kindness (1 Sam. 20:14–17).[1]

David learns that there is a surviving son of Jonathan (and grandson of Saul) named Mephibosheth, who is crippled in both feet because of an injury suffered when he was a child (v. 3; 4:4). David sends for Jonathan's son, makes him rich by restoring his family's property, and makes Mephibosheth welcome at his table, which essentially means that he is to be treated as a member of David's family.

Mephibosheth is a most unlikely recipient of David's kindness. As a descendant of King Saul, Mephibosheth would have been a potential rival for the throne.[2] David had already had to fight one of Saul's sons, Ish-bosheth, for the right to rule over Israel (2:8–4:12). Typically, victorious kings would exterminate the offspring of the previous dynasty in order to prevent the possibility of a future coup (1 Kings 15:29; 16:8–13). Mephibosheth's grandfather, Saul, had done everything he could to kill David when he perceived him to be a threat. But David had sworn that he would not do what was customary. He here keeps his promise and shows kindness to Jonathan's son. The Hebrew word translated "kindness" in verses 1, 3, and 7 is *hesed*, which often is used to refer to the LORD's covenant lovingkindness to His people (Exod. 34:6–7; Deut. 7:7–9; Ps. 23:6). The fact that Mephibosheth was physically disfigured also made him an unlikely object of David's kindness. Kings preferred to be surrounded by beautiful people. Deformed people were presumed to be under God's curse (Lev. 21:18–21; John 9:1–2). David nevertheless shows him great kindness. Mephibosheth, in gratitude, humbles himself before David, acknowledging him as the rightful king (vv. 6, 8).

David's kindness rejected by the Ammonites (10:1–19)

According to the Law, Israel was to wipe out the peoples occupying Canaan, but to offer peace to neighboring lands (Deut. 20:10–18). David had enjoyed a good relationship with Nahash, the king of the Ammonites, but when he offers kindness to his son, Hanun, David's messengers are insulted and humiliated (vv. 1–5). David is forced into a war with his neighbor (vv. 6–8; Ps. 120:7). General Joab employs sound military tactics while also looking to the LORD for help (vv. 9–12). God gives the armies of Israel victory (vv. 13–19), though the Ammonites will only be fully subdued after a long war (11:1; 12:26–31). This section ends with David at his peak, both in power as a king and in piety as a man of God. Sadly, it is during this war with the Ammonites that David will fall into sin, and as a result the trajectory of his story will turn sharply downwards.

Where do we see Jesus in this passage?

King David is a type of His descendant Jesus, who is the true King of Israel. David's victories point to the ultimate victory of our Lord. His good government gives a foretaste of the perfect government which will come when Jesus reigns.

Jesus is the LORD's anointed warrior King who has come to

crush the serpent and the forces aligned with him. "The Son of God appeared for this purpose, to destroy the works of the devil" (1 John 3:8b). He has come to reclaim the kingdom of this world for God, who has given it to Him as His inheritance (Ps. 2:8; John 8:54). God is with Jesus in all He does (8:6b). He conquers His enemies, making a public display of them (8:2; Col. 2:13–15; Heb. 2:14–15). Every enemy will be defeated (1 Cor. 15:24–25). He takes the spoils of war from among the devil's captives (8:4; Matt. 12:28–29). The territory He conquers extends beyond the borders of Canaan to the ends of the earth (Rom. 4:13; Acts 1:8; Ps. 72:8). The nations will come to Him offering tribute (8:6; Isa. 60:5; Micah 4:1–4; Rev. 21:26). He reigns in perfect wisdom and righteousness (Isa. 9:7; 11:1–5; Jer. 23:5–6). His kingdom will last forever (Rev. 11:15). Every person must make a choice of whether to fight against Jesus or to submit to Him (Ps. 2:10–12). Like King Toi, lay down your arms and submit to God's anointed King (8:10). Turn to Him and be saved (Ps. 72:12–13).

> Every person must make a choice of whether to fight against Jesus or to submit to Him.

David's lovingkindness to Mephibosheth is a picture of the LORD's kindness to us. We, like Mephibosheth, are the most unlikely objects of God's favor. Our father Adam, like Saul, lost the kingdom God had given him because of his sin. We, because of our sinful father, were born enemies of God, under a sentence of death (Rom. 5:12–14). Sin has marred us and God's image in us has been distorted (9:3b; Rom. 3:10–18). We are the undesirables of the world (1 Cor. 1:26–29). But the

LORD graciously sought us when we were hiding from Him (Isa. 65:1). We were spiritually lame, unable to come to God (John 6:44; Rom. 8:6–8). But the LORD showed lovingkindness to us for the sake of another who kept the covenant on our behalf (9:7; 1 John 2:12; 4:10). He invites us, though we were far off, to come to Him (9:5; Matt. 11:28–29; Eph. 2:13). He adopts us as sons who sit at His table (9:7b; Rom. 8:15–16, 23; Gal. 4:5; 1 John 3:1; Rev. 3:20). He restores to us the domain lost by our father Adam and makes us co-heirs with Him (Rom. 8:17; Eph. 1:11).

How does this passage apply to us?

David's aggressive foreign policy is not an example for rulers today because there is no nation or political entity which is a theocracy in covenant with God and is authorized to wage war on His behalf. Jesus explained that, under the New Covenant, His kingdom is not earthly and political, but spiritual (John 18:36). Not even the modern state of Israel is a theocracy because the kingdom was taken away from them because of their rebellion against the LORD (Matt. 21:33–44).

We are, instead, engaged in spiritual warfare. "For our struggle is not against flesh and blood, but against the rulers, against the powers, against the world forces of this darkness, against the spiritual forces of wickedness in the heavenly places" (Eph. 6:12). Like David, we are surrounded by hostile enemies—the world, the flesh, and the devil. We do not fight with literal swords but with the spiritual armor of God—truth, righteousness, the gospel, faith, salvation, the Word of God, and prayer (Eph. 6:10–20). We battle against sin, error, and unbelief (2 Cor. 10:4). We, through the gospel, seek to release captives from every nation so that they can join Christ's kingdom. Like David, we fight in God's strength and give Him the glory for our victories (8:6, 11, 14; Phil. 4:13; John 15:5; 1 Cor. 1:31). Though the battle belongs to the LORD, we, like David, are responsible to exert effort and use wisdom as we fight. We rejoice that victory is assured because our great anointed King has fought and won the victory for us (Matt. 16:18; Rom. 8:37).

As we, like Mephibosheth, have received such undeserved kindness from the LORD, we should be humble and grateful (9:6, 8). We also ought to reflect the LORD's lovingkindness in our relationships as we show grace to those who don't deserve it (Eph. 4:31–32; Matt. 5:43–48; Rom. 13:8).

We should also follow David's example in keeping our promises. David kept his commitment to Jonathan, even though Jonathan was dead and there was no one who could enforce his agreement. Marriage is the most important earthly covenant most of us make. Marriage vows typically include a commitment to remain faithful to each other "for better, for worse, for richer, for poorer, in sickness and in health, until God, by death, shall part us." Hard times test our character and commitment (Matt. 19:6). It is not enough, however, merely to avoid divorce. When getting married, we promise not just to remain married but to "love, honor, and cherish." Because marriage is the union of two sinners, much grace is required on both sides. We are able to love because we have first experienced the love of Christ (1 John 4:19). The same principle applies to the other commitments we make in life—in business, in friendship, and so on. The righteous man "swears to his own hurt and does not change" (Ps. 15:4c; see also Eph. 4:25; Matt. 5:33–37).

FOR FURTHER STUDY

1. What was Israel's foreign policy under the Old Covenant (Deut. 20)?

2. What was the justification for such aggression against other nations? Was David guilty of war crimes?

3. How do David's actions as a holy warrior point us to Christ?

4. Why was Mephibosheth a most unlikely recipient of King David's kindness?

5. Contrast Hanun's response to David's offer of kindness with that of Mephibosheth.

6. How does David measure up to the expectations for the ideal ruler in Deuteronomy 17:14–20?

7. How do the Ammonites portray what happens to those who reject God's offer of lovingkindness?

TO THINK ABOUT AND DISCUSS

1. Some today claim to engage in "holy war." What is the difference between what David did and what modern-day "holy warriors" are doing?

2. What is the nature of the warfare in which we are engaged? What does that imply for how we should approach this warfare?

3. Go through the armor of God in Ephesians 6:10–20 and discuss how each piece helps you in your battle.

4. How does David's faithfulness in keeping his commitment to Jonathan instruct us about how we need to keep our covenants and promises?

5. In what ways are we like Mephibosheth?

6. How can we reflect God's lovingkindness in our relationships as David did in his?

7. This section concludes with David at the height of his powers. Why are we most vulnerable when our lives appear to be going well?

8. Are we sometimes safer during times of trial than during times of ease? Explain your answer.

5 David's catastrophic sin

(11:1–27)

We have come to one of the most tragic chapters in the entire Bible. We have followed David's life from his youth, when he was an obscure shepherd boy, to his becoming the ideal king who has made Israel great while giving glory to God.

By faith, he conquered Israel's enemies, including Goliath. He was the man after God's own heart and the sweet psalmist of Israel. Yet now, in his later years, David acts like a typical Middle Eastern tyrant as he steals his neighbor's wife and then murders her husband as part of the cover-up.

This tragedy has been repeated many times among the leaders of God's people. Well-respected preachers have been caught in extra-marital affairs with women who were under their spiritual care.[1] Other well-known leaders have shaken the evangelical world by turning away from their marriages to a homosexual lifestyle. Such moral failures often take place in mid-life. And it is not just sexual sin of which our leaders have been guilty, but also scandalous financial misconduct, anger, domestic abuse, substance abuse, laziness, and pride. Neither is it just the leaders. There are numerous less-famous cases of professing Christian men and women acting disgracefully.

This chapter is so heartbreaking that we almost want to skip over it quickly. But I thank God for recording this incident in His perfect Word. The Bible, unlike other religious books, is brutally honest about its heroes. Noah got drunk. Abraham lied and put his wife's purity at risk. Moses became murderously angry. Peter denied Jesus. We want to look to mere men as our heroes, but God tells us not to put our ultimate trust in men, but to trust in Him (Jer. 17:5–8). This passage also serves to warn each of us against sin and presumption. "Therefore let him who thinks he stands take heed that he does not fall" (1 Cor. 10:12). David was a true believer who deeply loved God, yet even such a man can fall. We too are "prone to wander." No matter how long you have been a Christian, how much you have done for the Lord, or how mature you are in the faith, you will not be safe until you are in Christ's presence.

This passage is also valuable because it instructs us about how temptation works so that we might be able to resist and escape. This account, along with what is recorded in the following chapters, accurately portrays the ugliness and the consequences of sin so that we might be warned. This is a most helpful reminder for those of us who live in a culture which glorifies certain sins, especially those of a sexual nature.

Perhaps the most beneficial aspect of this tragic story

is that it points us to the gospel of Christ. When David is forgiven, we are reminded that there is hope for the worst of sinners who repents (Ps. 32; 51). Even those who have been sexually immoral or have committed murder (or abortion) are offered a way back to God, who offers forgiveness to repentant sinners.

Finally, the failure of David, the best king Israel could produce, reminds us that no earthly hero will suffice. In 1 Samuel God's people were looking for a worthy leader. Eli, Samuel, and Saul all fell short. In 2 Samuel Israel finally gets the leader for whom they have longed, but even David falls short. We need a king greater than David. Only Christ can fulfill that need.

David falls into sin (vv. 1–5)

Sometimes a large tree is blown down by what seems to be a moderate wind. Usually when this happens it is because the tree, which might have looked outwardly healthy, was rotting on the inside, thus making it vulnerable. David does not fall suddenly into sin. There were harbingers of David's fall. For example, rather than enjoying intimacy with one wife, David had acquired many wives for his own power and pleasure, in violation of God's design for marriage between one man and one woman (3:2–5; 5:13; Gen. 2:18–25; Matt. 19:4–5). God had explicitly forbidden kings to multiply wives (Deut. 17:17). Polygamy undermines the personal intimacy God designed for marriage between one man and one woman. David's degraded view of women influences him to see Bathsheba not as a person, but simply as an object to gratify his lust.

David's season of kingly success apparently also puts him off his guard. Prosperity can be dangerous, leading us to disregard God (Prov. 30:8–9). David was more spiritually secure when he was running for his life, and thus desperately seeking God (as he wrote about in the Psalms). He became ungrateful to God and failed properly to value God's blessings (12:7–9). What a sad contrast this scene is to his joyful worship when the ark of the covenant entered Jerusalem (6:14).

> David was more spiritually secure when he was running for his life, and thus desperately seeking God.

David is also guilty of neglecting his duties as king. The language is very vivid: "Then it happened, in the spring, at the time when kings go out to battle …" (v. 1a). David prematurely took off his armor and sent General Joab out to fight the Ammonites while he stayed in Jerusalem. He was in greater danger in his palace, outside the will of God, than on the battlefield, where he would have been fulfilling his calling.

David's fall into sin follows the progression described by James: "Each one is tempted when he is carried away and enticed by his own lust. Then when lust has conceived, it gives birth to sin; and when sin is accomplished, it brings forth death" (James 1:14–15).[2] Sin occurs because of temptation which lures us, not from the outside, but from within our own hearts (Mark 7:18–23).

First, David, while walking on the roof of his home, sees beautiful Bathsheba bathing, probably on the roof of her home (v. 2). At that time in the Middle East, homes would have a flat roof which would often be used as another room in the house[3] which could be a refuge from the heat. Apparently, Bathsheba was performing the ceremonial washing after her monthly cycle (which would be important later to prove that her husband Uriah, who was off to war, could not be the father of her child). David notices that Bathsheba is a beautiful woman (ironically, the same word was used to describe David's appearance in his youth, 1 Sam. 16:12). Temptation often comes through the "eye-gate" (1 John 2:16). Eve was tempted when she "saw that the tree was good for food, and that it was a delight to the eyes" (Gen. 3:6).

At this point David could have chosen to look away and to move on, since this woman did not belong to him (Matt. 5:27–30). He could have remembered the incident when Joseph ran from sexual temptation (Gen. 39:12; 2 Tim. 2:22). Instead he allows sinful desires to be conceived in his heart as he moves from looking to entertaining lustful thoughts about this bathing woman, and then inquires about her (v. 3a). The answer which David receives should stop him in his tracks (v. 3b). She is a married woman, and therefore not eligible to join his harem. To lie with her would be a violation of the seventh commandment (Exod. 20:14). Her husband is one of his loyal soldiers, among the "mighty men" who are presently fighting on King David's behalf (23:39). Her grandfather, Ahithophel, is one of David's key advisors. In spite of all this, the sinful desire which has been conceived in David's heart gives birth to the tragic act of sin. He sends for Bathsheba and takes her (v. 4). He abuses his royal power by using his servants as accomplices in his sin and by summoning Bathsheba, who, as a loyal subject, would be very reluctant to refuse the king.

The description of their sin is very brief. This is not some great romance. Afterwards, Bathsheba goes home after what appears to be a "one-night stand."

We might ask whether Bathsheba also bore some responsibility. She probably should have been more careful about her modesty, realizing that she could be seen on the roof (1 Tim. 2:9). Even though she was in a position of weakness, she still should have refused David's advances. Deuteronomy 22:22–24 teaches that a woman should cry out for help when a man tries to lie with her. Later, her husband Uriah was not afraid to stand up to the king (v. 11); she should have done the same.[4] But, as we will see in Nathan's parable of the ewe lamb, the blame falls primarily on King David, who abused his position of power and trust.

Finally, the sin brings forth its deadly consequences. Bathsheba is pregnant (v. 5). "Be sure your sin will find you out"; "whatever a man sows, this he will also reap" (Num. 32:23; Gal. 6:7). The conception of a child, which should be an occasion for great joy, is seen as a tragedy. Bathsheba could be stoned to death as an adulteress. David could be exposed as an adulterer who is worthy of death (Deut. 22:22; Prov. 6:32–33; 7:22–27). As a result of David's sin, many will die or suffer other harmful effects of his transgression. David touched not only Bathsheba. He also touched her husband, her father, her grandfather, his own family, and even the nation.

David's deadly cover-up (vv. 6–27)

Sinners have always tried to cover up their sin, beginning with the fig leaves worn by Adam and Eve (Gen. 3:7–8). David is so eager to appear to be a righteous man that he is willing to lie and even to kill to maintain his reputation.

First, David attempts to make it appear that Uriah is the unborn child's father (vv. 6–13). David summons Uriah from the battle under the pretense that he wants a report about the state of the war against the Ammonites. David then encourages Uriah to go home to enjoy his respite from battle by lying with his wife, Bathsheba. When her pregnancy was revealed, Uriah would then be the presumed father. But Uriah refuses the pleasure of his wife's bed because his duty is with the army of God which is engaged in holy war. Uriah has the courage to obey God rather than men (Acts 5:29). He is one person whom David cannot control by his kingly power. David, who should have been convicted to the point of repentance by this man's devotion to the very duties he himself has neglected, then tries to make Uriah drunk so that he will lie with Bathsheba. Again David's plan for a cover-up fails.

David then resorts to even more drastic measures. In our day an unwanted pregnancy is often terminated. In this case it is the husband whom David terminates. He arranges, with the help of General Joab, for Uriah to die in battle. David can then marry Bathsheba, thus making the unborn child appear to be legitimately his (vv. 14–25). David even makes Uriah carry his own death warrant (v. 14).

David has now sunk to the level of tyrants like Saul who abuse their power and viciously eliminate their rivals. David had previously been very critical of Joab's ruthlessness (3:26–39), but now he sinks to Joab's level as he uses his unscrupulous general for his own despotic ends.[5] Uriah, who was willing to die for his king, does indeed die because of his king. David, who had been appointed to smite the LORD's enemies, smites the LORD's faithful servant and gives the LORD's enemies cause to blaspheme (12:14). After Uriah's death David mutters a platitude about the perils of war (v. 25) and then quickly marries the widow Bathsheba (vv. 26–27a).

It appears that David's cover-up has worked. But the LORD has noticed the evil he has done and He will deal with it in due time (v. 27b). David is not in control after all. The consequences of his sin will be far-reaching and lifelong (12:10–14).

Where do we see Jesus in this passage?

This passage shows that we need someone greater than David to be our King. David fell under temptation. Jesus was tempted in all ways as we are, yet without sin (Heb. 4:15). David became the king who took what was not his. Jesus is the King who gives to those who do not deserve it. Jesus comes to the aid of sinners, first by providing a way through His sacrifice for us to be forgiven (1 John 1:8–2:2; 1 Peter 3:18), and then by helping us to fight temptation (Heb. 4:16; 2:18; 1 Cor. 10:13). No matter what your sin, Jesus is able to help you. When we study the sin of David we should be most thankful for Jesus!

How does this passage apply to us?

Beware of spiritual presumption. We may be safer during times of trial than during times of ease. David was better off spiritually when he was being chased by Saul and had to hide in a cave than when he was secure as king over Israel. Just because you have been walking with the Lord for a long time and have been greatly used by Him, it does not mean that you cannot fall (1 Cor. 10:12; 1 Peter 5:8). Guard your heart (Prov. 4:23) and your eyes (2 Tim. 2:22; Job 31:1). Looking upon and thinking about what God has forbidden, whether in sexual temptation, substance abuse, or covetousness, allows lust to be conceived in your heart. You must control your thoughts (Phil. 4:8–9) and keep yourself away from influences, including entertainment, which might turn your heart in the wrong direction. Just as a tiny embryo in a mother's womb gradually and inevitably grows until she gives birth to a fully formed baby, so a hidden embryonic desire will ultimately give birth to an act of sin which brings death (James 1:14–15). We also learn, from Bathsheba's bad example, that we need to be careful not to act or dress in such a way (i.e. immodestly or flirtatiously) which could cause others to stumble into temptation.

> **Keep yourself away from influences, including entertainment, which might turn your heart in the wrong direction.**

This story also reminds us of the deceitfulness of sin (Heb. 3:13) as we can convince ourselves that the pleasure of sin is worthwhile and that we can somehow get away without any serious consequences. The reality is that sin is enslaving (John 8:34) and destructive (Gal. 6:7). One transgression often leads to many others. David didn't break just the seventh commandment (adultery). He also neglected his vocation (violating the fourth commandment[6]). He coveted his neighbor's wife (tenth commandment). He murdered (sixth commandment). He stole his neighbor's wife (eighth commandment). He lied and deceived (ninth commandment). He made an idol of his own desires (first and second commandments). He gave the LORD's enemies cause to blaspheme (third commandment).

The lying and the cover-up are often more destructive than the act of adultery itself. In many cases of marital unfaithfulness we often hear, "I might be able to forgive the sexual sin, but I don't know if I can ever trust this man again. He has been living a lie." When someone commits adultery (or another serious sin) there are usually many other accompanying sins, including lying/deceit (Eph. 4:25), stealing/wasting money, putting others at risk (e.g. the innocent spouse at risk of sexually transmitted diseases), and so on. In our day, Bathsheba's pregnancy would be considered "unwanted." Just as David took the life of Uriah because of an unwanted pregnancy, so today many unborn babies are murdered because of sexual sin.

Just as David's sin with Bathsheba affected a multitude of other people, so our sin, while primarily against God, also negatively impacts many people. The person with whom you sin is someone's spouse, brother/sister, child, grandson/daughter, friend, and so on. Our children, our parents, our in-laws, the people in our church, the people with whom we work, and our neighbors are all affected when we slide into scandalous sin. What begins with an inappropriate glance at something on the Internet (where temptation abounds) or a flirtatious comment on social media can lead to life-altering sin.

Positively, the best way to avoid sinful desires is to cultivate a greater and higher desire for the Lord. We should not only flee lust, but also "pursue righteousness, faith, love and peace, with those who call on the Lord from a pure heart" (2 Tim. 2:22). If you are walking closely with God you will not be so vulnerable to temptation. Joseph was able to resist Potiphar's wife because he was most concerned about his relationship with the LORD (Gen. 39:9). Christ offers you higher and greater pleasures than any temptation. He is more satisfying than any fleshly sin (Isa. 55:1–2). It is also important to remember who you are in Christ. Your old self has died with Him and now you are a new person united with Him in His resurrection (Rom. 6:11; Col. 3:5). Learn from David, who fell when he was neglecting his calling, and stay busy fulfilling God's calling on your life (Col. 3:23). Idleness is very dangerous (1 Thes. 5:7). Many get into spiritual trouble when they waste hours watching television or surfing the Internet when they should be busy being fruitful for the Lord.

Another way to resist sexual temptation is to pursue God's ideals for love and intimacy in every aspect of your marriage (Eph. 5:22–33; Prov. 5:15–23) and to respect the marriages of others.

Finally, if you have started to give into temptation, abort your embryonic sin before it gives birth to death (James 1:14–15). At every stage David could have chosen to turn away from his sin, but he kept moving toward destruction. Take radical action to kill your sin before it kills you (2 Tim. 2:22; Matt. 5:29). Seek godly accountability (Heb. 3:13). The longer you wait, the greater will be the consequences you will face. You can hide your sin from man, but you can never fool God. Pray that God will give you a tender conscience (Ps. 139:23–24) and will grant you complete repentance.

FOR FURTHER STUDY

1. Why did the LORD tolerate polygamy during the Old Testament era?
2. What made David vulnerable to temptation at this particular time in his life?
3. How does David's fall into sin follow the progression described in James 1:14–15?
4. Was Bathsheba guilty? Or was she merely a victim of David's sin?
5. Why is it ironic that Bathsheba ceremonially purified herself after lying with David (11:4)?
6. Of what sins, other than adultery, was David guilty?
7. How were others affected by David's sin?

TO THINK ABOUT AND DISCUSS

1. When a person in authority puts sexual pressure on a subordinate, is it abuse?
2. What blame does the subordinate bear when he or she gives in?
3. What safeguards do you need in your life to prevent a serious fall into temptation?
4. How should we respond to unwanted pregnancies (11:5)?
5. How would you answer someone who says that sex is a private matter which involves only two people?
6. Write down a list of the consequences if you were to fall into sexual sin.
7. How does Uriah set a positive example for us?

6 The LORD confronts David's sin

(12:1–31)

Several months have passed since David's fall into adultery with Bathsheba and murder of Uriah. While there may have been some whispers among those in the palace (or among those who could count to nine months), David appears to have gotten away with his sin. He remains secure on his throne.

But the king is in a terrible place spiritually (see Ps. 32:3–4). The worst thing for David would be for the LORD to abandon him in his sin (as had happened to wayward King Saul). Instead, the LORD takes notice of David's sin (11:27b) and shows his great love for him by sending the prophet Nathan to expose and confront David's sin so that the king might be led to repentance. This is also the story of how the LORD restores many straying believers, and how He uses us to help restore one another.

The LORD sends Nathan to David (vv. 1–12)

David is hiding from the LORD, who therefore sends His

prophet to pursue his wayward king (v. 1a). We already met Nathan in chapter 7, when David sought to build a temple for the LORD. Nathan's job that day was pleasant as He was the LORD's mouthpiece through whom David was told of the great covenant blessings which would come upon his house. This time Nathan is given a much more difficult assignment. It is dangerous to confront a king. "The terror of a king is like the growling of a lion. He who provokes him to anger forfeits his own life" (Prov. 20:2). John the Baptist was later put to death for rebuking King Herod for his sexual sin. The fact that a prophet of the LORD could confront the king of Israel in this way was a reminder that God Himself was the true King over His people, including their king.

Nathan uses a parable to get past David's defenses (vv. 1b–4).[1] The story of the ewe lamb is appropriate in light of David's previous career as a shepherd of literal sheep and his present responsibility as the shepherd-king of Israel (5:2; 1 Sam. 16:11). Nathan's parable is wonderfully crafted to fit the situation. David is the rich man who had his own herd (harem of wives). Uriah is the poor man with but one beloved lamb (wife). The traveler probably represents David's sexual appetite which he could have legitimately satisfied with one of his own wives. Instead, David abuses his power by stealing the poor man's beloved ewe lamb.

David reacts to Nathan's story with righteous anger (vv. 5–6). Even though his conscience has been hardened, he still has a strong sense of right and wrong. David, in condemning the rich man, unknowingly pronounces sentence upon himself.

Nathan then boldly proclaims, "You are the man!" (v. 7a).

He then follows the typical pattern of the prophets who would function as God's lawyers in a covenant lawsuit. David is reminded of God's faithfulness to him (vv. 7b–8). The LORD had greatly blessed David by elevating him from obscurity to be king over all Israel. He delivered David from his enemies and made him rich in possessions and wives. Then the king's own faithlessness is exposed (v. 9). David, by his acts of adultery and murder, has shown contempt for the LORD Himself and has given the LORD's enemies cause to blaspheme (v. 14). Finally, the LORD reveals the consequences of covenant disobedience (vv. 10–12).

David repents and the LORD forgives (v. 13; Ps. 51; 32)

David's response to Nathan's rebuke stands in stark contrast to the proud self-centered response of former King Saul after he was rebuked by Samuel (1 Sam. 15). Many people show worldly sorrow when they are caught in a great sin, but true repentance is rare, especially among powerful men and women (2 Cor. 7:10–11). David's psalms of repentance demonstrate that his heart was truly broken because of his sin (Ps. 32; 51).

> Against You, You only, I have sinned
> And done what is evil in Your sight,
> So that you are justified when You speak
> And blameless when you judge …
> Hide Your face from my sins
> And blot out all my iniquities.
> Create in me a clean heart, O God,
> And renew a steadfast spirit within me.

Psalm 51:4, 9–10

After David's confession, the LORD, through Nathan, pronounces forgiveness (v. 13b). Though the Law demands that David die for his crimes (Lev. 20:10; 24:17; Deut. 22:22), his life is spared and his kingdom is not taken away. The New Testament, quoting from Psalm 32, tells us that David's guilt was removed by means of faith which looked ahead to the atoning work of Christ (Rom. 4:5–8). God is very gracious toward repentant sinners (Isa. 1:18; Ps. 32:5; 103:10–12).

David still suffers the consequences of his sin (vv. 14–23)

Though David is forgiven, he will endure the consequences of his sin for the rest of his life (as is recorded in the rest of 2 Samuel). The son born to Bathsheba will die (v. 14), in spite of David's fasting and prayers (vv. 15–23). David's punishment fits his crimes (Exod. 21:24). Just as he destroyed another man's house through adultery and murder, so his house will be ravaged by sexual sin and murder (vv. 10–12). Four of David's sons will die premature deaths (v. 18; 13:29; 18:14–15; 1 Kings 2:24) and there will be shameful sexual immorality. What David tried to hide in his own life will be exposed for all to see through his sons. The sword will not depart from David's house as there will be rebellions and civil war in Israel (v. 10).

The LORD again shows kindness to David (vv. 24–31)

The LORD blesses David and Bathsheba with another son in the place of the child who died (vv. 24–25). David names the child Solomon, which speaks of God's peace (shalom). The LORD, through the prophet, gives the child another name, Jedidiah, which means "beloved of the LORD." Even though this marriage began in a very sinful way, the LORD's blessing again rests on David and his offspring.

The LORD also blesses David with a decisive victory over the Ammonites (vv. 26–31). The story has come full circle as David finally joins and wins the battle he had sinfully avoided (11:1).

Where do we see Jesus in this passage?

Just as the LORD sent Nathan to restore David, so Jesus seeks us out and restores us when we wander. He will not let any of His sheep perish (7:14; John 10:27–29).

David's sinful failure reminds us how much we need Jesus. It is only when we understand how vile our sin is that we appreciate the greatness of His work in saving us. He paid a great price on the cross so that we could be justly forgiven of our guilt (Isa. 53:6). Our sin, like David's sin, is forgiven by the atoning sacrifice of Christ (Rom. 3:21–26). The sacrifices of David's day could not actually remove sin (Heb. 10:4), but pointed forward to Jesus' work on the cross. Through Christ our guilt is carried away (Ps. 32:1a). Our iniquity was laid upon Him (Ps. 32:2; Isa. 53:5–6, 11). Jesus provides the cleansing for which David longed (Ps. 51:7; Heb. 1:3). His atoning blood covers our guilt (Ps. 32:1; Heb. 9:14; Isa. 53:8), so that our sins are no longer counted against us (Ps. 32:2a; Rom. 5:8; 2 Cor. 5:21).

But just as David could only be forgiven when he confessed his guilt, so the forgiveness of Christ only comes to those who repent of their sin and turn to Him in faith (1 John 1:8–9). The fact that God could forgive David after he had committed adultery and murder is a precious reminder of the greatness of His mercy and grace toward sinners like us. God still forgives repentant sinners. There is no sinner beyond the reach of His grace (1 Cor. 6:9–11).

How does this passage apply to us?

A real Christian can get into a terrible spiritual state. We are tempted to hide from God during such times—avoiding fellowship, putting on an act in front of others that everything is OK, not reading Scripture, nor praying. Thanks be to God that He pursues and disciplines His children (Prov. 3:11–12; Heb. 12:5–11). Though true believers may fall into sin, He will not allow them to remain in sin. He cannot forget His love for us (Isa. 49:14–16). The LORD's process of disciplinary restoration may be hard and unpleasant, but in the end it is good and beneficial. "Before I was afflicted I went astray, but now I keep Your word" (Ps. 119:67).

> Though true believers may fall into sin, He will not allow them to remain in sin.

Those who are caught in their own sin still have a sense of justice and can become very angry at the sins of others (12:5–6; Matt. 7:1–5). We can be very sensitive to the sins of others while easily overlooking our own. For example, I have counseled men who are abusive, selfish, indulge in pornography, and are guilty of substance abuse, yet who will erupt in judgmental anger against a wife who is not completely obedient (often quoting Scripture—Eph. 5:22, but not Eph. 5:25).

The LORD still uses human messengers to confront and

restore His wayward people. Church leaders are called pastors (shepherds), which reflects their special duty to seek out wandering sheep (1 Peter 5:1–5; Acts 20:28). God calls upon every believer to do what Nathan did in restoring wayward brothers and sisters. "Brethren, even if anyone is caught in any trespass, you who are spiritual, restore such a one in a spirit of gentleness; each one looking to yourself, so that you too will not be tempted. Bear one another's burdens, and thereby fulfill the law of Christ" (Gal. 6:1–2; see also Matt. 18:15–20; Heb. 10:24; Rom. 15:14; James 5:20; Prov. 27:5–6; Lev. 19:17). Those who offer correction need to be careful that they are walking in the Spirit and not according to the flesh (Gal. 6:1; 5:16–26). Also, we should remember that it is much easier to receive correction from someone who loves you and is trying to help you than from someone who is venting his or her anger. We must go humbly (because we too are sinners who need grace) and gently (because we remember how hard it is to be corrected). We must also be sure that we have dealt with our own sins (removed the beam from our eye) before addressing the sins of others (Matt. 7:1–5). We should carefully choose the time and manner in which we address our brother or sister's sin (Prov. 25:11–12). Nathan, rather than going straight to the king with his accusation, wisely helped David to form his own conclusion. Our goal in confronting sin is not to condemn our brother or sister, but to

> Those who offer correction need to be careful that they are walking in the Spirit and not according to the flesh.

restore him or her to God (Gal. 6:1). We are all to be brother-keepers. It can take special bravery to confront a person who is powerful or has a strong personality. Confronting sin is dangerous because not every sinner responds as well as David ultimately does. We need to overcome our own fear of man as we trust in the LORD (Prov. 29:25). Sometimes love demands that we speak.

Do you welcome correction from others? "Do not reprove a scoffer, or he will hate you. Reprove a wise man and he will love you" (Prov. 9:8). When someone tries to rebuke us we can be tempted to defend ourselves or to make counter-accusations ("You aren't so great yourself"). Even if the person who approaches us does not do it perfectly, we should listen carefully. God may have sent him or her to rescue us. In our culture, which tolerates and even celebrates sin and selfishness, we all need people who love us enough to speak truth into our lives. "Faithful are the wounds of a friend, but deceitful are the kisses of an enemy" (Prov. 27:6). Some powerful people, including pastors, lack accountability because no one can safely get close enough to admonish them. It is all too common that a person in authority, when receiving correction, erupts in anger and accuses the subordinate of disloyalty.

Sin is taken much too lightly in our day. People presume that they can do as they wish (including what David did) and that God will forgive them. I once heard a professing Christian say that she would, without biblical grounds, divorce her husband, knowing that God would forgive her. Even when sin is forgiven, serious consequences may remain. David admitted his sin and was forgiven, but he and his family experienced the bad fruit of what he sowed. Learn from David that you cannot defy God and come out ahead.

> I will instruct you and teach you in the way which you should go;
>
> I will counsel you with My eye upon you.
>
> Do not be as the horse or as the mule which have no understanding,
>
> Whose trappings include bit and bridle to hold them in check,
>
> Otherwise they will not come near to you.
>
> Many are the sorrows of the wicked,
>
> But he who trusts in the Lord, lovingkindness shall surround him.
>
> Psalm 32:8–10

Many see sins such as adultery primarily on the horizontal plane—how they affect other people. This passage reminds us that our sin is primarily against God. Though many people were affected by what David did, his greatest transgression was against the Lord (12:9, 14; Ps. 51:4).

God shows undeserved kindness to repentant sinners. Though David and Bathsheba's union had a sordid beginning, the Lord blessed them with a son who would one day be king. God still shows mercy by blessing marriages which may have had a very bad or even an immoral beginning.

We who have, like David, been forgiven much should be willing to forgive others as God has forgiven us (Eph. 4:32; Matt. 18:21–34; 6:12).

FOR FURTHER STUDY

1. Why was it dangerous for Nathan to confront David?

2. According to God's Law, what should have happened to David? Why didn't it happen?

3. Why does the Lord speak only of David's sin against Him, without mentioning David's sins against Bathsheba and Uriah?

4. Why was the parable of the ewe lamb such an effective way for Nathan to confront David?

5. How are parables like that of the ewe lamb used elsewhere in Scripture?

6. How was it just that David's infant son, who wasn't guilty, should die (12:14)?

7. Does 2 Samuel 12:23 teach that infants who die go to heaven?

TO THINK ABOUT AND DISCUSS

1. When have you experienced the Lord's discipline? How did you benefit?

2. Nathan was sent by the Lord to confront King David. How can you know if the Lord wants you to confront a wayward brother or sister?

3. Do we have the right and duty to confront those in authority over us (e.g. a child going to a parent, a wife to a husband, or a church member to a pastor)?

4. How well do you receive correction?

5. Do you have anyone like Nathan in your life—someone who has the courage and freedom to correct you even when you are running from the truth?

6. What is the difference between true repentance and worldly sorrow (2 Cor. 7:10–11)?

7. Does the fact that David was allowed to continue to rule as king after committing adultery mean that a pastor who has committed adultery can continue in the ministry (1 Tim. 3:1–7)? Explain your answer.

8. When we forgive others, must we always remove all the consequences of their sin? Give examples of when it is appropriate to remove consequences and when it is not.

9. Do you humbly submit to the Lord's will when He says "no" to your prayers (12:19–23)?

10. Can God still bless a marriage which began sinfully, such as after an unbiblical divorce?

7 David's chastisement continues: Amnon, Tamar, and Absalom

(13:1–39)

If 2 Samuel 11 is one of the most tragic chapters in Scripture, 2 Samuel 13 is as sordid as any story in the Bible. There is deceit, rape, incest, vengeance, fratricide, and family estrangement. The Word of the LORD to David through the prophet Nathan is being fulfilled: "I will raise up evil against you from your own household" (2 Sam. 12:11). David reaps in his children what he has sowed through his own sin (Gal. 6:7).

This chapter addresses issues which are all too common in today's church—lust, sexual abuse, wayward children, and broken family relationships. There are people in our congregations who have been sexually assaulted. There are families whose adult children have done shameful things and brought them great grief. There are young people who don't know the difference between lust and love. The Word of God offers valuable instruction and hope.

Amnon rapes his half-sister Tamar (vv. 1–19)

Amnon, who is David's oldest son and the heir apparent (3:2), finds himself attracted to his beautiful half-sister Tamar (13:1; 3:3). He is frustrated because, as she is his sister, she is forbidden to him under the Law (Lev. 18:9, 11). Amnon's passion for Tamar is so great that he is afflicted both emotionally and physically (v. 2). Amnon is following in the tragic footsteps of his father, David. He is attracted to a beautiful woman who is off-limits (11:2–3; Matt. 5:28). Rather than fleeing from temptation, he indulges his desires, which leads to further sin which has deadly consequences (13:4; James 1:14–15).

Amnon's cousin Jonadab tells Amnon just what he wants to hear, affirming that the prince has the right to be happy and to have whatever he desires. His advice ignores the LORD and his Law and encourages Amnon to act like the princes among the pagan nations. Jonadab then hatches a clever plot by which Amnon can, by pretending to be ill, be alone with his sister so that he can have his way with her (vv. 3–5). Jonadab's plot is both evil and shrewd, taking advantage of the sympathy and trust of David and Tamar.

Amnon carries out Jonadab's plot. He persuades his father David to send Tamar to care for him in his supposed illness (vv. 6–7). Unsuspecting Tamar obeys her father and goes to her brother, who takes hold of her and propositions her (vv. 8–11). Tamar's pleas are heartbreaking as she begs Amnon not to bring disgrace upon himself and reproach upon her.

She encourages him to instead pursue marriage honorably (vv. 12–13). Amnon is beyond persuasion or even shame, and he rapes her (v. 14).

At this point, the only decent thing for Amnon to do would be to marry Tamar (Exod. 22:16–17; Deut. 22:28–29). Instead, this tale becomes even sadder as Amnon, having taken away Tamar's purity, then hatefully rejects her (v. 15).[1] This proves that what Amnon thought was love (v. 1) was really selfish lust. Again Tamar pleas for him to act honorably, but Amnon casts her out[2] as if she is a common prostitute (vv. 16–17). Amnon has followed in the footsteps of his father, David, who also abused his power to get what he wanted, to the destruction of others. Tamar cries out in her desolation (vv. 18–19; Deut. 22:24). Will anyone care for her?

King David fails to enact justice (v. 21)

Tamar has been left desolate, having been wickedly violated and cast off by her half-brother Amnon. She does not hide her grief, but cries out. Tamar's cry is a call for justice (v. 19; see Gen. 4:10; Exod. 2:23). Her father, King David, has been appointed by God to enact divine justice, both as the head of the family and as the head of state (1 Peter 2:14; Rom. 13:4). David becomes angry, but he does nothing. He should have defended Tamar's honor and punished Amnon for his disgraceful sin. David seems to be like Eli, who was upset about the scandalous sins of his sons but failed to act (1 Sam. 2:22–25). Eli was rebuked because he honored his sons above the LORD (1 Sam. 2:29). David seems to share Eli's fault of failing to deal with evil in his own house. When later another son, Adonijah, is on the verge of stealing the throne from Solomon, we are told, "His father had never crossed him at any time by asking, 'Why have you done so?'" (1 Kings 1:6). Later we will see that David had also indulged his son Absalom. Perhaps David's own moral failures made it hard for him to judge the sins of his sons. David's inaction also indirectly led to Absalom's murder of Amnon and Absalom's rebellion against David. Perhaps this is the moment when Absalom lost all respect for his father and began to view himself as a more worthy king. "Because the sentence against an evil deed is not executed quickly, therefore the hearts of the sons of men among them are given fully to do evil" (Eccles. 8:11).

Absalom takes murderous revenge against his half-brother Amnon (vv. 20, 22–39)

When David fails to act, Absalom begins to assume the role of leadership in the family by taking Tamar into his home (v. 20). He bides his time as he waits for the opportunity to avenge his sister's loss of honor (v. 32), perhaps luring Amnon into a false sense of security (vv. 22–23). All the while, poor Tamar remains desolate (v. 20b). Absalom does what David failed to do by punishing Amnon for his crimes.

There are many parallels between how Tamar is tricked into being alone with her half-brother Amnon, who rapes her, and how Amnon is lured into being alone with his half-brother Absalom, who murders him (vv. 24–29). In each case the perpetrator takes advantage of a trusting victim's sense of family duty (vv. 6, 26); in each case David sends his child to his or her doom (vv. 7, 27); and in each case David is upset, but does not take action (vv. 21, 36). There are also parallels between Amnon's death and David's murder of

Uriah, including the fact that both victims are got drunk (v. 28; 11:13); both perpetrators use underlings to carry out the vile deed (v. 29; 11:15–17); and David receives a report from a messenger after each deed is done (vv. 30–33; 11:18–24).[3] It is ironic that Amnon, who had manipulated trusting Tamar into a rape, is lured by his trusted brother to his own murder.

Absalom, after killing Amnon, flees and remains separated from his father, David, for three years (v. 38). After Amnon's murder, David again appears to be a weak and indecisive king. He mourns over his dead son Amnon, tearing his robe; but why didn't he mourn for his daughter Tamar, who tore her robe (vv. 31, 19)? The estrangement between David and Absalom will lead to David's next big problem as Absalom emerges as a rival to the throne. Absalom is handsome and cunning, and he commands great loyalty. Furthermore, he is bitter against his father and no longer respects him. Soon Absalom will try to stage a coup.

David is responsible for all these calamities. The man who was once the righteous and wise ruler has become indecisive and has failed to execute justice for the oppressed. He is out of touch and outwitted. Was one night with Bathsheba worth all this?

Where do we see Jesus in this passage?

Where King David miserably failed, Jesus succeeds. He is the protector and comforter of the oppressed (Ps. 68:5; 146:9; Prov. 31:9). Even when human justice fails, He will judge those who oppress others (Ps. 9:7–9; Rom. 12:19). Jesus is able to sympathize with the victims of abuse because He was abused for us (Ps. 22:6; Isa. 53:7). He sets an example for victims of abuse as he entrusted Himself to God and did not take his own revenge (1 Peter 2:23). He also offers sympathy and help to those who have been sorely tried (Heb. 4:15–16).

In contrast to the false love/lust of Amnon, Jesus has loved us with a sacrificial purifying love (Eph. 5:25–30; John 15:13). He removed our shame and disgrace on the cross (Isa. 53:4).

Jesus also frees us from bondage to sinful desires, even those practiced by our forefathers (1 Peter 1:18–19; Ezek. 18:14–18). Even if your father was like David or even Amnon, the gospel can set you free (Titus 3:3–5).

How does this passage apply to us?

We learn from Amnon that what is called love is often nothing more than lust (vv. 1, 15). He did not want Tamar as a companion in a lifelong covenant of marriage with whom he could build a family. He simply wanted to use her as an object for his own sexual gratification. Young people may feel a strong attraction or passion for someone which can be misinterpreted as love. True love seeks what is best for the other person and is willing to sacrifice self-interest for the good of the other, just as Christ gave Himself for us. True love is expressed within the bounds of God's Word, because no one gains by defying the LORD.

> True love seeks what is best for the other person and is willing to sacrifice self-interest for the good of the other.

We also see, from the case of Amnon, that sin never satisfies. He spent a long time dreaming about being with Tamar and exerted great effort plotting their union. But once it happened, it didn't meet his expectations and he had no more use for her. Amnon, like his father, David, also reminds us that sin brings terrible consequences in our lives and in the lives of others whom our sin affects.

Jonadab's example warns us of the danger of wicked friends and counselors (1 Cor. 15:33). They may flatter us by telling us what we want to hear (Prov. 29:5). "He who walks with wise men will be wise, but the companion of fools will suffer harm" (Prov. 13:20). You will be influenced by the company you keep. Friends like Jonadab, even if they seem very charming and clever, are enemies to your soul who encourage you to gratify the flesh rather than walk in the Spirit.

There is much we can learn from Tamar. Many women long to be beautiful, but outward beauty can be a mixed blessing. Tamar possessed such beauty (v. 1), but the result was that it attracted a man who was only interested in her appearance and not in her person (Prov. 31:30). Tamar, in many ways, positively exemplified the inner beauty of a woman of God. She honored her father (vv. 7–8). She was willing to work with her hands (v. 9; Prov. 31:13). She showed mercy to those in need (v. 10; Prov. 31:20). She feared God and was morally pure (vv. 12–13; Prov. 31:30). She wisely resisted sexual temptation, deploring fornication because it violates God's holy law (v. 12), harms others (v. 13b), and would harm herself (v. 13a). She respected marriage as the only proper place for sexual expression (v. 13c; Heb. 13:4). Tamar is also a reminder that terrible things may happen to the righteous in this life (1 Peter 2:21). Our hope is for the life which is yet to come.

Tamar's scenario is repeated in many families and churches today. There are too many women in our congregations who can identify with the misery and shame which flooded Tamar's soul. A man who desires a woman who is off-limits finds a way, through deceit, to get her alone. The man, the stronger person, takes advantage of the weaker woman, selfishly using her to gratify his sexual desires. She is then left in her devastated state. Those who should protect her fail to act, and even participate in the cover-up, thereby multiplying her pain and shame. Our churches need to note the following points in order to face the threat of sexual abuse:

- Sexual predators are incredibly deceitful. Like Amnon, they manipulate circumstances and other people to get alone with a trusting young person and then take advantage of him or her sexually.
- Potential victims need to be taught to cry out (Deut. 22:24). Because sexual predators are masters of manipulation, boys and girls need to be prepared at a very young age to know exactly what to do if someone acts inappropriately toward them. Many victims are naïve and vulnerable. Often when sexual abuse takes place, the female victim is ashamed and keeps what happened to her a secret. She is often manipulated by the perpetrator, and sometimes by family members who don't want a public scandal. Often she is blamed because of the way she acted or dressed. Women need to cry out so that the perpetrator can be identified and so that other women can be protected. If previous victims

had cried out, the sexual offender might have been stopped before he got to you (Matt. 7:12).

- We need to take the cries of the oppressed seriously, offering protection and help. After Tamar was raped by Amnon, her father, King David, was very angry (v. 21) but did nothing. Even her brother Absalom told her, "Has Amnon your brother been with you? But now keep silent, my sister, he is your brother; do not take this matter to heart" (v. 20). Many victims are told to keep silent in order to avoid disrupting the family or the church community. Yet Scripture teaches that we are to reflect God's particular care for the weak and the oppressed (Prov. 31:8–9; Ps. 146:7). In many cases, if those who were aware of an abuser's evil acts of the past had taken action, he or she would have been stopped decades earlier. Failure to enact justice has terrible consequences. Often, when one case of abuse is exposed, many other victims come forward.

- Sexual predators need to be publicly exposed. A well-known denomination was scandalized following the exposure of the practice of moving priests who were sexual predators from one parish to another (where they would then find more victims). In the same way, many families choose to hide the crimes of a predatory grandfather or an uncle in order to avoid the disruption and shame which would result from their exposure. The same cover-ups have happened in churches and Christian organizations. Church leaders and others who abuse their position of power and influence must be dealt with publicly (1 Tim. 5:19–20), and, where appropriate, their crimes must be reported to the governing authorities (Rom. 13:4; 1 Peter 2:14). Spiritual leaders who abuse their power to take sexual advantage of others are permanently disqualified from leadership (1 Tim. 3:1–7), no matter how gifted or effective they may seem to be. The cover-ups must end.

• Victims need help to deal with the past biblically. In his excellent book, *Putting Your Past in Its Place*,[4] Steve Viars speaks of how when we are sinned against we can respond either righteously or unrighteously. While the predator has the far greater sin, the victim may be guilty of responding sinfully to what has happened to him or her. Some victims fail to cry out. Some victims, after initial resistance, become willing participants in sexual sin. The victim needs to understand that he or she has, like Bathsheba and Tamar, been sinned against by a person who abused his or her position of power. The victim may also need to confess his or her personal sin to God and to others who have been affected by the sin. On the other hand, many victims feel false guilt and shame. Tamar did nothing wrong. The perpetrator bears the guilt for his or her assault and deserves to be disgraced before God and man.

We can also learn from David how our sinful example may influence our children. Matthew Henry writes, "Parents know not how fatal the consequences may be in any instance they give their children bad examples."[5] David was guilty of being an indulgent parent who failed to allow his children to suffer the consequences of their sins. Sadly, parents continue to walk in David's and Eli's footsteps (1 Sam. 2:29; Prov. 13:24). Not all waywardness in children is the fault of their parents, however. Matthew Henry writes, "Godly parents have often been afflicted with wicked children; grace does not run in the blood, but corruption does. We do not find that David's children imitated him in his devotion; but his false steps they trod in, and in those did much worse and repented not."[6] The LORD Himself has wayward children (Isa. 1:2).

David's failure to protect Tamar reminds us that parents have a special responsibility to protect their daughters (and sons) and that those in authority have a duty to enact justice swiftly. We are also reminded that when the proper authorities fail to act, vigilantes will often take justice into their own hands.

FOR FURTHER STUDY

1. Why did Tamar tear her clothes and cry after she left Amnon? Wouldn't her future prospects have been better if she had tried to cover up what had happened to her?

2. Is there significance to the fact that the LORD's name is never mentioned in this chapter?

3. Why does God allow such terrible things to take place?

4. How was the LORD working out His plan through these terrible events?

5. What should David have done when he heard what Amnon had done (Lev. 20:17; Exod. 22:16)?

6. Was Absalom's murder of Amnon just? Why or why not?

TO THINK ABOUT AND DISCUSS

1. What harm results when parents are indulgent with their adult children?[7]

2. Is it the parents' fault when children, like Amnon and Absalom, do evil?

3. Amnon said that he loved Tamar (v. 1). What is the difference between true love and base lust?

4. How do men today often act like Amnon in their relationships with women?

5. What harm results when leaders of families, churches, and governments fail to enact justice?

6. Absalom took personal revenge on his brother (v. 32). Why shouldn't we take revenge against those who wrong us or do great evil (Rom. 12:17–21)?

7. How can we help victims of sexual abuse or trafficking?[8]

8 Trickery, treachery, and treason

(14:1–16:14)

Many have experienced estrangement within their families such that grown children no longer communicate with their parents or one sibling will no longer attend family events if another particular sibling is going to be there. David experiences estrangement with his son Absalom, and this then degrades into civil war in Israel.

All this is the consequence of his great sin with Bathsheba (12:10–11). In the midst of this family crisis, the once-great king is portrayed as passive and weak. When his sons do great evil, David is unwilling to take steps to enact justice. As his kingdom is crumbling, rather than being the master of the events in Israel, David seems to be overwhelmed by circumstances and dependent upon others to move events forward by taking decisive action.

Absalom is allowed to return to Jerusalem (14:1–33)

After Absalom murders his half-brother Amnon, he spends three years in a self-imposed exile (13:38). Absalom desires to return to Jerusalem and David wants him to come home (13:39), but nothing is done. David's general, Joab, who is a man of action, shrewdly takes steps to bring about Absalom's return. He sets up a situation in which a widow appears before David pleading for the king's intervention to bring her estranged family back together after one of her sons has killed the other (vv. 1–6). Other family members are demanding that the guilty son die, but if this happens the widow will be alone and destitute (v. 7). David responds to her pleas by declaring that her son can live (vv. 8–11). David, at this point, probably expects her to leave as a loyal and grateful subject. Instead, the widow springs her trap and reveals her real purpose, which is (on Joab's behalf) to persuade David to let his banished son return to Jerusalem, just as the king was willing to let her banished son safely return to her (vv. 12–17). David finally recognizes that he has been manipulated by Joab, but he does allow Absalom to return to Jerusalem (vv. 18–23).

Joab's story, told through the widow, is very similar to Nathan's story of the ewe lamb. Rather than addressing the situation directly, Joab gets the woman to tell a kind of parable which arouses David's sympathy. Both stories call upon David to carry out his kingly function by bringing justice for the oppressed (Ps. 68:5). In both incidents David is maneuvered into condemning himself when he pronounces judgment on a guilty third party. And in each case the storyteller's objective is realized.

We are told that Absalom looks like a king (vv. 25–27), a fact which serves to increase his popularity among the people (who are influenced by such things, 1 Sam. 10:23; 16:6–7). We are also told about Absalom's children, including a daughter named Tamar (v. 27), presumably after his half-sister who was raped by Amnon (and probably as a reminder of David's failure to enact justice).

David, however, remains unwilling to give Absalom a personal audience (v. 24), which probably further embitters his son. Absalom finally resorts to arson in order to manipulate General Joab to persuade his father, the king, to receive him (vv. 27–33). Again, David appears weak and indecisive as he only takes action when others force him to do so. What are Absalom's motives for seeing his father? Is he really seeking his father's love and acceptance? Or is he using the audience with the king as a stepping stone to advance his own ambition to steal the kingdom?

Absalom's conspiracy (15:1–12)

After Absalom manipulates Joab and his father into letting him return to Jerusalem, he manipulates the people of Israel to shift their loyalty from David to him. By pomp and show he creates a popular public persona (v. 1). He also steals the hearts of the people by claiming that he will be a more just and attentive leader than his father (vv. 2–4) and by flattering his future subjects (vv. 5–6; Prov. 26:28).

Just as Absalom had patiently waited for an opportune time to carry out his plot to murder his brother Amnon, so he waits for the right moment to carry out his shrewd plan treasonously to steal his father's throne. David, again the ineffectual and naïve king, allows Absalom to go to Hebron under the pretext of worship (vv. 7–9). Absalom then sends loyal messengers throughout the kingdom proclaiming that he is king (v. 10). He also brings two hundred unsuspecting noblemen with him (v. 11); they will then either join his conspiracy or be kept from offering David the help he will need in such a crisis. And Absalom enlists the wisest man in Israel to be his advisor (v. 12a). The tide of public opinion is turned toward Absalom. Apparently, they are ready for a new king (v. 12b). Implicit in Absalom's rebellion is his determination that his father (and brothers) must die so that he can occupy the throne without fearing any rival.

David's flight and David's friends (15:13–16:14)

David reaches a low point when he has to run for his life in order to escape being assassinated by his son Absalom and the multitude who have joined his conspiracy (15:13–14). A relatively small remnant of the people remains faithful to David and accompanies him as he departs from Jerusalem (15:15–18). David encounters other loyal friends as he flees. Ittai the Gittite is an unlikely ally, being a Philistine from Goliath's hometown of Gath, but apparently, like Ruth the Moabitess, he is determined to follow David, even to death (15:19–23; Ruth 1:16–17). It appears that, like Ruth, Ittai is not merely following David but the LORD. Zadok and the other priests also remain loyal, but David instructs them to remain with the ark of God in Jerusalem (15:24–25).[1]

David humbly submits his future to the will of God

(15:25–26). He also takes steps to secure his future. He instructs Zadok to be his eyes and ears in Jerusalem after Absalom arrives (15:27–28). This spy work will provide vital information for the king (17:15–22). As David humbly departs the city he learns that his close advisor Ahithophel has betrayed him by going over to Absalom's side (15:30–31; Ps. 41:9).[2] David prays that Ahithophel's counsel will be confounded and then takes steps toward that end by sending Hushai the Archite to serve as a spy who might undermine the advice of Ahithophel (15:32–37; 17:1–14).

David also has some negative encounters during his flight from Absalom. He encounters Ziba, who claims that Jonathan's son, Mephibosheth, to whom David had shown such kindness (9:1–13), has betrayed the king in his hour of need (16:1–3). David judges Mephibosheth and rewards Ziba (16:4). This later will appear to have been a rash action. "The first to plead his case seems right, until another comes and examines him" (Prov. 18:17; see also Prov. 18:13, 15). David also encounters former King Saul's relative Shimei, who curses the king, claiming that David richly deserves the evil which has come upon him through Absalom (16:5–8, 13). David resists the impulse of his hot-headed but loyal soldier Abishai, who wants to kill Shimei on the spot (16:9–10).[3] Instead David humbles himself and hopes that the LORD will reward him for his forbearance (16:11–12). Later, after David, against all odds, prevails, the terrified Shimei will claim to be repentant (19:16–23), though years later he will be punished by Solomon (1 Kings 2:8–9, 36–46).

David reaches the Jordan, exhausted after a hard journey of over twenty miles, and humbled (16:14). All this is still the consequence of David's great sin. On the positive side, after a long period of inaction and indecision, it seems that David is again starting to act like a king as he prepares for battle. He also explicitly acknowledges the Lord's hand in his trials and puts his hope in Him (15:26–27; 16:11–12).

Where do we see Jesus in this passage?

David's darkest hour foreshadows that of Jesus. Both passed by the Mount of Olives and the Kidron (15:23, 30; Luke 19:37; 22:39; John 18:1). Just as David was betrayed by those he had saved in battle and served as king (15:13), so King Jesus was rejected by His own people (John 1:11) and betrayed by someone he loved (Ps. 41:9; John 13:18; Luke 22:21). Jesus, like David, sought to protect his remaining loyal followers (15:20; John 18:8), and restrained them from taking revenge upon those who cursed Him (16:10–12; Matt. 26:51–54). "While being reviled, He did not revile in return; while suffering, He uttered no threats, but kept entrusting Himself to Him who judges righteously" (1 Peter 2:23). Jesus, like David, was wearied in his suffering and humiliation (16:14; John 19:28). As in David's case, Jesus understood that His suffering was according to God's plan (12:11; 16:11–12; Luke 22:29; 24:26; Isa. 53:10; Acts 2:23). Jesus, when He was being betrayed by those who sought to kill Him, submitted Himself to the Father's will (15:25–26; Luke 22:42).

Unlike David, Jesus did not suffer for his own sin, but for ours (12:10; 1 Peter 2:24; 3:18). Unlike David, Jesus did not escape death. Like David, Jesus, after his humiliation, was brought back again to glory because the Lord delights in Him (15:25; 16:12; Matt. 27:43; Acts 2:24).

The people of Jerusalem were fair-weather friends to King David (15:6, 12; 19:8–10). Jesus too has fair-weather friends who abandon Him when times are hard. Are you a faithful friend to Jesus? Will you, like David's few loyal friends, stand with and follow Jesus, even when all seem to be against Him (Mark 8:34; 1 Peter 4:12)?

How does this passage apply to us?

David is again a tragic picture of a man who is reaping what he has sowed (Gal. 6:7). He is also a weak, indecisive, and indulgent father and king. His leniency with his wayward sons brings yet more grief and trouble to himself and to his kingdom (Prov. 29:15b; 17:25).

Absalom serves as a warning of what can happen when a son receives no correction (Prov. 19:18). He is another example of a man who misuses his many earthly advantages, which include shrewdness, good looks, and leadership ability. Proverbs warns us against flatterers who manipulate others for their own purposes (Prov. 29:5). Politicians make promises they never intend to keep in order to get strategic interest groups to vote for them. Absaloms have even been known to arise in the churches. They steal the hearts of God's people by claiming that the present leadership is falling short and that they would surely do a much better job running the church (15:4–6). While they may accurately criticize the weaknesses of others, they rarely prove to be more effective as leaders.

At first it seems shocking that the people who had been so blessed with victory, prosperity, and peace during David's reign so quickly turned to the traitor Absalom (15:12b). But such is fickle human nature. Winston Churchill was voted out of office as Prime Minister shortly after leading Great Britain through World War II. Both John Calvin and Jonathan Edwards were rejected by ungrateful congregations. People will let us down or even betray us. The Apostle Paul was abandoned by those who should have stood by him (2 Tim. 4:16–17). We cannot put our ultimate trust in mankind, but only in the LORD, who will never leave us nor forsake us (Jer. 17:5–8).

On the other hand, some domineering church leaders have misused the story of Absalom's treason as a way to accuse anyone who questions their authority of sinful treason against the Lord. David is a type of Christ (not any human pastor in our day), the One to whom our ultimate loyalty belongs. Scripture teaches that our leaders need to be held accountable, and, if necessary, disciplined when they are in sin or error (1 Tim. 5:19–21; Gal. 2:11–14).

> We cannot put our ultimate trust in mankind, but only in the LORD, who will never leave us nor forsake us.

At this point in the story, it seems that Absalom's conspiracy was succeeding. We often see people getting away with evil in business, in government, and in religion. Sometimes we may feel that everything is against us. Trust that God will act in due time. Absalom will illustrate that, while the wicked may prosper for a season, the LORD has ordained that they will be judged in the end (Ps. 73).

David also offers us a positive example as he humbled himself before God and submitted to His will (15:25–26; 16:10–11). God offers us hope and grace, even when our trials are of our own making, when we humbly repent before Him (Isa. 55:6–7). David, by his restraint, also set a godly example of what we should do when others slander us (16:9–12). We too may face Shimeis. We can trust God to deal with them and we can also seek to learn what He may be teaching us through this difficult experience. David also demonstrates, as he has in the past, that it is good both to pray and to take appropriate strategic action which is in accordance with our prayers (15:31–36). You may pray for good things such as a job, a spouse, or an opportunity for ministry and evangelism. After praying, don't merely sit around waiting for an answer to drop from the sky, but take appropriate action employing the means which might lead to your desired ends.

FOR FURTHER STUDY

1. Why did Joab allow himself to be manipulated by Absalom?

2. How was the widow's story like Nathan's story of the ewe lamb (14:1–20)?

3. Why did David flee from Jerusalem? Couldn't he have trusted God to help him stay and fight?

4. David said that he submitted his future to the will of the LORD, but he also took many strategic steps to ensure his own survival. Was there any inconsistency between David's words and actions?

5. Why was Ittai the Gittite an unlikely man to be following David (15:19–23)? How was he like Ruth?

6. Why didn't David use the ark in battle against Absalom?

7. How was David's darkest hour like that of Jesus?

TO THINK ABOUT AND DISCUSS

1. How do wayward adult children manipulate their parents with religion today (15:7–9)?

2. How do political and religious leaders today operate as Absalom did?

3. Do those who are critical of their present leaders prove to be capable of doing a better job?

4. What are some examples of people being fickle toward those to whom they should be loyal?

5. Are you ever guilty of making quick judgments without hearing all the facts (16:4; Prov. 18:15, 17)?

9 Victory, judgment, and grief

(16:15–18:33)

It seems that everything is against David. His son Absalom has stolen the hearts of the people and his kingdom. David has had to flee for his life. Absalom is accompanied by Ahithophel, whose advice appears to be infallible. Evil seems to have won the day.

Sometimes we can feel that everything is against us. The forces of evil in our nation and in the world seem to be growing stronger. Christians are being mistreated and even persecuted. Perhaps we can also be tempted to feel hopeless and bitter about circumstances in our own lives. Yet we, like David, should never forget that the LORD is in control. We can put our hope in Him (15:25).

The battle before the battle (16:15–17:29)

As Absalom enters Jerusalem in triumph, David's friend (and spy) Hushai greets him. When Absalom questions his loyalty, Hushai answers with cleverness and guile: "As I have served in your father's presence, so I will be in your presence" (16:19b). Absalom succumbs to this flattery and so Hushai infiltrates Absalom's inner circle of advisors, where he will continue to serve David just as he said (16:15–19).

Absalom then turns to Ahithophel, who counsels him to assert his royal power by lying with the women of the king's harem (16:20–22). Such an insulting act toward his father makes reconciliation with David impossible (Gen. 35:22; 49:3–4). This immoral outrage is in fulfillment of the judgment Nathan pronounced upon David: "I will raise up evil against you from your own household; I will even take your wives before your eyes and give them to your companion, and he will lie with your wives in broad daylight. Indeed you did it secretly, but I will do this thing before all Israel, and under the sun" (12:11–12). Ahithophel, like Jonadab (13:3), is evil but very shrewd (16:23). Absalom's grip on the kingdom is tightened.

Ahithophel then advises Absalom to complete the coup by quickly striking David (17:1–4). Ahithophel offers to lead a medium-sized force of 12,000 men whose sole objective will be the death of David. Once the king is gone, there will be no one left behind around whom the opposition can rally, so the people will follow Absalom. There is only one factor which brilliant Ahithophel forgets: "Many plans are in a man's heart, but the counsel of the LORD will stand" (Prov. 19:21).

While Absalom likes Ahithophel's plan, he decides to seek a second opinion from Hushai (17:5–6). Hushai cleverly undermines Ahithophel's plan by playing on Absalom's fears and David's reputation as a fighter (17:7–10). He then appeals to Absalom's vanity by proposing that Absalom

himself lead a great army against David and his followers
(17:11–13). Hushai's plan buys time for David to prepare
for battle. Absalom chooses Hushai's plan over that of
Ahithophel. Why didn't Absalom just follow Ahithophel's
excellent plan rather than seeking Hushai's advice, which
was doomed to fail? "For the LORD had ordained to thwart
the good counsel of Ahithophel, so that the LORD might
bring calamity on Absalom" (17:14b; see also Prov. 21:1, 30).
Ahithophel, in his great foresight, realizes that Hushai's plan
is doomed and commits suicide (17:23). David's prayer that
Ahithophel's counsel be thwarted has been answered (15:31;
Ps. 55:23). The battle of the advisors in 2 Samuel 17, won by
Hushai, will determine the outcome of the war between the
armies in 2 Samuel 18.

Hushai then activates the rest of the spy network, having
the priests send their sons to warn David, who is able to move
to safety and prepare for battle (17:15–22). Again we see the
hand of God as Jonathan and Ahimaaz escape capture (much
as the spies were rescued by Rahab in Jericho in Josh. 2).
David is helped by three loyal friends who incur significant
expense and risk their own lives (Absalom would probably
kill them if he prevailed) by caring for David and his men
in their hour of great need (17:27–29). Later, after David
prevails, they are rewarded (19:31–39). Both armies then
take their positions to fight the one great battle of Absalom's
civil war (17:24–26).

Civil war in Israel (18:1–33)

David prepares his men for battle by dividing the troops
among his three generals (vv. 1–2). Again we see that while

the LORD gives the victory, human responsibility through strategy and effort are the means He uses. David's men insist that David not put himself at risk by entering the battle (vv. 3–4). Ahithophel was right: this war is like a game of chess. The army which takes down the other side's king will win. Finally, David charges his generals to spare Absalom's life (v. 5), again exposing his weakness for his wayward sons. Absalom is seeking to destroy David's kingdom. Because of him, thousands of lives will be lost. He is an incorrigible son who deserves to die (Deut. 21:18–21). So long as he lives, there can be no peace in Israel. Yet David ties the hands of his generals.[1] He is out of touch with the realities of war and is more sentimental than wise. David is also opposing the purpose of the LORD, who has determined that Absalom must die (17:14).

The description of the battle is very brief. David's men prevail with the help of the LORD (vv. 6–8). The main point of this story is what happens to Absalom. This arrogant rebel is caught in a tree and suspended by his hair, of which he had been so proud (v. 9; 14:26). When an unnamed soldier, out of respect for David's order, refuses to strike Absalom down, ruthless Joab willingly does the deed (vv. 10–15). David's evil son meets an accursed end (vv. 17–18; Deut. 21:23). With Absalom's death the war ends (v. 16).

Joab sends a messenger to David, who is anxiously awaiting news (vv. 19–27). Yet the king's chief concern is not for his own throne or for the men who risked their lives for him in battle. All he seems to care about is his wicked son (vv. 28–32). When David learns of Absalom's death he is overcome with grief. "O my son Absalom, my son, my son Absalom! Would I had died instead of you, O Absalom, my son, my son!" (v. 33). David's excessive grief puts his kingdom at risk (19:1–7).

Where do we see Jesus in this passage?

Just as David was betrayed by his close advisor Ahithophel, so our LORD was betrayed by one of his disciples, Judas (15:31; 16:23; Ps. 41:5–9; 55:12–14; John 13:18; 18:2; Matt. 26:14–16). Just as Ahithophel counseled Absalom to steal the kingdom by killing David the anointed king, so Jesus' enemies thought they could keep their power by killing Jesus Christ (Matt. 21:38; John 11:50–52; Acts 4:24–28).

> Even when all seems lost from a human perspective, God accomplishes His purposes.

Even when all seems lost from a human perspective, God accomplishes His purposes. Just as God sovereignly thwarted Ahithophel's plan, so through the resurrection He thwarted the plans of those who killed the Lord Jesus (Acts 2:23–24; Ps. 41:10–13). David won the civil war and again reigned on the throne of Israel. Jesus reigns even after death. Both betrayers, Ahithophel and Judas, took their own lives (17:23; Matt. 27:1–5; Acts 1:18–20, 25).

Just as David's friends helped him in his time of great need and at great personal risk and cost (17:27–29), so Jesus is our true Friend who at great cost met our need (2 Cor. 8:9). Just as David's friends willingly served God's anointed king, so we should gladly serve Christ, even if we pay a price for our loyalty. In the end we, like they, will receive a great reward.

Mankind, like the people of Israel, has rejected God's King and enthroned another (Satan) who deceitfully promises us better things (Gen. 3:1–6). As a result we are under a curse, just as Absalom was. Jesus came and was also hung on a tree, not for his own sins (like Absalom), but to bear our curse (Gal. 3:13; Deut. 21:23). Jesus, like Absalom, had a spear thrust into Him (18:14; John 19:34). Just as David sought to do good to a son who hated him, so Jesus did good for His enemies (Luke 23:34; Rom. 5:6–10). Just as David sorrowed over the fate of his wayward son (18:33), so Jesus wept over the unbelief of His people (Luke 13:34; 19:41).

Unlike David, Jesus is able to bring the prodigals home (Luke 1:17; 15:11–32).

How does this passage apply to us?

Just as the LORD worked in spite of Ahithophel and Absalom, so God is still working out all things for the good of those who love Him (Rom. 8:28). He still brings judgment on evildoers (Ps. 73:16–20). He is sovereign, even over evil rulers who disregard or hate Him (Prov. 21:1). It is futile to try to thwart His purposes (Prov. 21:30; 16:1, 9). Because God is the ultimate power in the world, we don't need to fear men (Prov. 29:25).

Hushai delivered David by deceiving Absalom. There are other examples in Scripture in which people mislead others or lie in what appears to be a good cause. Through deceit, Rahab hid the spies in Joshua 2 and the midwives protected the babies in Exodus 1. There are also examples in Scripture in which subterfuge is used in war (Josh. 8). In light of the ninth commandment (Exod. 20:16) Christians debate whether it is ever permissible to lie. Some would argue that Rahab, the midwives, and Hushai should have trusted God to provide a way of deliverance without compromising truth. Others have concluded that while we owe our brothers and our neighbors the truth, we do not owe truth to our enemies (e.g. those who are trying to kill us in war).[2] Either way, we can conclude that when someone lies to us, that person is treating us as an enemy. Falsehood destroys families, churches, and friendships (Eph. 4:25). If there is such a thing as righteous lying, it is very rare.[3]

Ahithophel's pitiful end illustrates how a person may be very smart and gifted, but if he or she doesn't honor the Lord, that person's life is a failure. Ahithophel, like others who take their own lives, committed suicide because he had no hope for the future. Those who reject God's anointed one have no hope, but God offers grace to those who will return to Him (Isa. 55:6–7).

David's loyal friends, who were willing to risk their lives to help God's anointed king, exemplify the compassion and care we should have for those in need (17:27–29; Rom. 12:10, 15; 1 John 3:17–18) and the nature of loyal friendship (Prov. 17:7).

David's concern for Absalom, which exceeded the care he had for his loyal followers and for the will of God, serves as a warning to parents. A man can have a tender affection for his children and still raise them poorly, especially when he, like David and Eli, is more concerned about keeping his sons happy than pleasing the Lord (1 Sam. 2:29).

The poignant picture of David weeping over Absalom is a reminder that many parents grieve deeply over their wayward children. Jesus warned that loyalty to Him would divide families (Luke 12:51–53). Spurgeon writes, "Our children may plunge into the worst of sins, but they are our children still … but at the same time, we cannot unchild them, nor erase their image from our hearts."[4] We gain some comfort from the fact that God Himself knows what it is like to grieve over rebellious sons. "Listen, O heavens, and hear, O earth; for the Lord speaks, 'Sons I have reared and brought up, but they have revolted against Me'" (Isa. 1:2; see also Jer. 2:30).

Absalom serves as a monument of warning to rebellious children who proudly turn from the Lord and dishonor their parents (Exod. 20:12; Prov. 20:20; 30:17). The Lord will bring judgment upon proud and defiant young adults who refuse to repent (Ps. 92:7–9). He has many branches which stretch out for rebels (18:9).

For further study ▶

FOR FURTHER STUDY

1. What are some other examples in Scripture of the Lord sovereignly controlling the heart of a ruler (17:14; Prov. 21:1; Rom. 9:17)?

2. In what other cases in Scripture do God's people deceive their enemies as Hushai deceived Absalom (Josh. 2; Exod. 1:18–20)?

3. How was Ahithophel like Judas?

4. What other suicides are recorded in Scripture (17:23)?

5. Was Joab justified in slaying Absalom (18:14)?

6. How was the death of Jesus like the death of Absalom?

TO THINK ABOUT AND DISCUSS

1. What are some examples of people in our day (in politics, business, and religion) who are, like Ahithophel, brilliant, but evil (16:23)?

2. Could it be said that Hitler's decision not to invade Britain, but instead to declare war on Russia, was evidence of the hand of God thwarting his plan?

3. Did Absalom choose Hushai's advice of his own free will? How does this relate to God's sovereignty over his decision (17:14)?

4. Was Hushai's deceit justified? When, if ever, are lying and deceit justifiable?

5. What harm does lying do to relationships (Eph. 4:25)?

6. How does Ahithophel's suicide (17:23) shed light on why people take their own lives?

7. How do parents today honor their children above God (18:33; 1 Sam. 2:29)?

10 Return of the king

(19:1–20:26)

After Absalom's rebellion is put down, King David returns to Jerusalem. In the aftermath of victory he deals wisely, both with his friends and with those who were his enemies. But other rebels lurk in the shadows waiting for any further sign of weakness from the king.

Joab again rescues David (19:1–8a)

As David continues to mourn over his son Absalom, ever-shrewd General Joab rebukes David for showing love to the murderous traitor while treating shamefully the loyal subjects who risked their lives to save him. Joab warns David that if he does not reach out to his followers, the kingdom which Absalom failed to take from him will be lost (vv. 1–7). David heads Joab's warning and holds court at the gate, where the people can come before him (v. 8). Even though Joab is often unscrupulous and ruthless, he remains loyal to David, acting in the king's best interests,[1] even in a situation in which he might have been able to seize power for himself.

David is restored to his throne (19:8b–15)

In the aftermath of civil war the divided nation must be healed. The northern tribes take the initiative to restore David as their king, recalling his past exploits (vv. 8b–10). Perhaps they should have wondered why they ever would have betrayed David by following Absalom. David rallies support in his home tribe of Judah and among the priests (vv. 11–14). Strangely, David elevates Absalom's general Amasa to replace Joab as the commander of his army, perhaps as an effort to unite the two sides after battle. This also could be retribution, because Joab had defied David's order to spare Absalom's life (18:5, 10–14). Amasa's time as commander of the army does not last long, however, as ruthless Joab takes the first opportunity to assassinate his successor (as he had killed General Abner years before, 3:27) and regain his position (20:9). The hearts of the people are again turned to King David.

David faces his foes and his friends (19:16–39)

As David was fleeing for his life he had some significant encounters. Now that he is back on this throne he meets with the same people again. Shimei, a loyalist to former King Saul, had bitterly cursed the king, probably under the assumption that David would soon be dead at Absalom's hands (16:5–8, 13). Imagine his dismay and fear when David emerges victorious! Rather than trying to flee for his life, however, Shimei rushes into the king's presence to beg for forgiveness

(vv. 16–20). The day of victory is often an opportunity for amnesty (1 Sam. 11:12–13). Though Shimei deserves to be put to death, David shows mercy (vv. 21–23). David may also be influenced by the fact that Shimei is a powerful man whose support would be most helpful.[2]

Then Mephibosheth, Jonathan's son to whom David had previously shown lovingkindness (9:1–13), approaches King David. His servant Ziba had accused him of treason, and so David had given Ziba his master's property (16:1–4). Mephibosheth claims that his loyalty has never wavered, and accuses Ziba of deceitfully leaving him behind when he wanted to go with David and then wickedly slandering him to the king (vv. 24–28). Mephibosheth's haggard appearance testifies to how distraught he has been over the king's plight. David, perhaps not knowing whom to believe, chooses to divide the estate between Ziba and Mephibosheth (vv. 29–30).

Finally, Barzillai, who, at great personal risk, had helped David in his hour of need, approaches the king (vv. 31–32). David wants to reward him for his faithful service, but Barzillai asks that Chimham (his grandson?) take his place. David's kindness to Barzillai continues through Solomon's reign (1 Kings 2:7).

Divisions among the tribes lead to another revolt (19:40–20:2)

The end of Absalom's conspiracy is not the end of David's troubles. Quarreling between Judah and the northern tribes leads to a revolt late in David's reign and foreshadows future longer-lasting divisions in Israel (19:40–43; see also 1 Kings 12). David's failure to lead wisely appears to stir up tribal loyalty and contribute to the problem (19:9–14). When the tribes bicker he doesn't appear to do anything to bring about peace and reconciliation.

Sheba, a worthless fellow (1 Sam. 2:12; 10:27; 25:17, 25), stirs the northern tribes to break away from David's kingdom (20:1–2). The people who had recently been claiming to have ten parts in David (19:43) again turn fickle and want no portion in God's anointed king (20:1). Again they break their covenant with David (5:3).

The rebellion is quickly put down (20:3–26)

David wants to act quickly against Sheba and sends Amasa to raise an army (vv. 4–7). Joab treacherously murders Amasa and resumes command of David's army (20:8–12). Joab lays siege to the city of Abel, where Sheba is seeking refuge. An unnamed wise woman (Eccles. 9:14–16) intervenes with Joab and persuades the people of the city to kill Sheba. Thus the city is saved and the rebellion ends (vv. 13–22). Another rebel comes under God's judgment and life in Israel returns to normal (vv. 23–26).

Where do we see Jesus in this passage?

We must put Christ and His kingdom above our families (Luke 19:26; 9:59–62). When we suffer great loss, including the loss of loved ones, we can trust Jesus to satisfy our souls (Jer. 17:5–8). Jesus will wipe away every tear (Isa. 25:8; Rev. 21:4).

Having defeated the usurper of His kingdom, Christ invites former rebels to draw near to Him in peace (Luke 19:10; Matt. 11:28–29).

Jesus, like David, restrains his followers from taking

revenge on his behalf (19:22; Luke 9:54–56; Matt. 26:51–54) and even rescues his enemies from the judgment they deserve (Col. 1:21). Shimei portrays how rebellious sinners should humbly and respectfully approach God's triumphant King, pleading for mercy. It is interesting that the language Shimei used with David is the same language David used to plead with God for forgiveness in his psalms of repentance (19:19–20; Ps. 32:2, 5; 51:2, 4–5, 7, 9).

How does this passage apply to us?

While it is appropriate to mourn over the loss of a loved one (Eccles. 3:4; 7:1; John 11:35), a believer's grief must be tempered by his or her duty to God (Luke 9:59–60). David mourned excessively and inappropriately over Absalom's death. There are few harder trials in life than the death of an unsaved loved one. In such a case we must be careful not to side against God. Aaron sets an excellent example as he remained silent when his sons were struck down under God's justice (Lev. 10:1–3). It is not God's fault (Ezek. 33:11; James 1:13–14), but the fault of the one who willfully rejects the LORD and chooses evil.

> While it is appropriate to mourn over the loss of a loved one, a believer's grief must be tempered by his or her duty to God.

David wisely responded to Joab's rebuke (19:7–8). How well do you receive correction (Prov. 9:8)?

Shimei's humble approach to David shows how we should seek someone's forgiveness when we are in the wrong (Matt. 5:23–26; 7:5). David's willingness to forgive is a picture of how we should show mercy to those who wrong us (Eph. 4:31–32; Col. 3:12–13; Luke 6:27–36; 17:3–4).

Assuming that Mephibosheth is telling the truth, it seems that David didn't do his kingly duty to carefully search out legal matters so that justice was enacted (Prov. 25:2; 18:17). There may be times in our lives when the authorities fail to enact justice in a legal matter or in the workplace. You may be in the right, but unable to prove it because it is your word against that of an effective liar. Or you, like David, may be in a position in which you hear both sides and are unsure who is telling the truth. Parents often face this difficulty with the quarrels of their children. Ultimately, we can trust God to bring about justice (Rom. 12:19).

Mephibosheth is a good model of how to deal with disappointments and injustices. In light of the fact that he had received grace when he deserved death, he realized that he had nothing to complain about (19:28; Rom. 6:23; Eph. 2:1–10). Furthermore, Mephibosheth was so pleased to be in the presence of the king that material things no longer mattered (19:30; Heb. 13:5). May we be so delighted in Christ that earthly losses mean little to us (2 Peter 3:11–13; 1 John 3:2) as we await His triumphant return (1 Cor. 16:22).

Barzillai exhibits many of the qualities of older saints which should be understood and appreciated by those of us who are younger. With age comes diminished capacity to enjoy worldly pleasures (19:35a). Some older people are worried about being a burden (19:36b) and want to remain in familiar surroundings (19:37a). They are often very aware that death is approaching (19:34, 37) and want to be a blessing to those who are younger (19:38). Barzillai in his old age makes a great (and probably painful) effort to be where the king is honored (19:31), just as many of our older people have to exert great effort in order to come to worship Christ with us. Older people can still do important things for the glory of God (Ps. 92:12–14) and should be honored among us (Prov. 16:31; 20:29). Those who are loyal to God's anointed King will be honored and rewarded.[3]

Just as the tribes of Israel unnecessarily quarreled over David (19:40–43), so unnecessary factions arise among Christians (1 Cor. 1:10–17; Gal. 5:15). Many divisions among us stem more from pride, personalities, and hurt feelings than matters of biblical substance. Harsh words, anger over perceived slights, impugning motives, defensiveness, and returning evil for evil can cause lasting breaches (19:41–43). Then, when people's feelings are hurt, they leave or split the church (20:1–2). Christians should be peacemakers (Matt. 5:9; Heb. 12:14; Rom. 12:18) who are willing to overlook perceived offenses (Prov. 19:11; 16:32; 1 Peter 4:8), assume the best of others (1 Cor. 13:7), and speak with kindness and grace (Prov. 15:1; Eph. 4:29). It is amazing that the church continues in spite of our sins, failures, and rebellions (Matt. 16:18).

For further study ▶

1. How are we to evaluate Joab's character in light of his loyalty to David and his ruthlessness (and willingness to go against orders)?

2. Why did David put up with Joab?

3. Compare David's response to the death of Absalom under God's judgment with that of Aaron when his sons died (Lev. 10:1–3) or Job's response when his children died (Job 1:18–22).

4. Why did David appoint Amasa as commander of his army (19:13)? Do you think this was a wise decision?

5. Did David fulfill his kingly duty to search out the matter between Mephibosheth and Ziba (Prov. 18:17; 25:2)? Would it have been possible for David to have definitively known the truth?

6. How were David's concubines victims of his sin (20:3)?

7. What other wise women have we encountered in 1 and 2 Samuel (20:16, 22)?

8. How does David's experience in this passage reflect the life of Christ?

1. How much sorrow is appropriate upon the death of a loved one? What is excessive mourning, and why is it wrong?

2. When a believer dies we have hope (Phil. 1:21; 1 Thes. 4:13–17), but how can we face the death of an unsaved loved one like David's son Absalom?

3. What would you say to a father under such circumstances?

4. How does Shimei's encounter with David exemplify how we should seek forgiveness from God and from one another? Is there someone whose forgiveness you need to seek?

5. Is there someone whom you must forgive?

6. What is to be done when someone in authority doesn't know who is telling the truth (19:28)?

7. How should we respond when we don't receive justice (19:29–30)?

8. How does Barzillai help us to understand many of the qualities of our older saints?

9. Is it ever good to have a Joab in the government or in the church?

10. How are the divisions in the church today like the divisions among the tribes of Israel (19:40–43; Gal. 5:15; 1 Cor. 1:10–17)? How can such divisions be prevented?

11 Hard times and heroes

(21:1–22; 23:8–24:25)

Most commentators regard 2 Samuel 21–24 as an epilogue or appendix to the book. While it appears that the incident described in 23:13–17 took place earlier in David's life, it is unclear when some of the other events occurred. This section also includes some events which are very difficult for us to understand.

There is a chiastic pattern in the epilogue (see page opposite).

The center of a chiasm (in this case, David's psalms, which we will cover in the final chapter) is often the most important part. This entire section portrays David as an ideal king who establishes a pattern for future kings of Israel.

Atonement for covenant-breaking (21:1–14)

The story of David avenging Saul's mistreatment of the Gibeonites is one of the most difficult in the Bible. Famine

1. King Saul's sin causes a famine which ends when atonement is made (21:1–14)

2. A list of heroes (David's mighty men) and their exploits (21:15–22)

3. David's song of praise to the LORD for His past faithfulness (22:1–51)

3. David's song of praise for the LORD's future faithfulness (23:1–7)

2. A list of heroes (David's mighty men) and their exploits (23:8–39)

1. King David's sin causes pestilence which ends when atonement is made (24:1–25)

strikes Israel, which brings great suffering to an agrarian people dependent upon rainfall for survival. David knows that droughts do not occur by chance in Israel, in light of God's promise to give them rain when they are faithful to the covenant (Deut. 28:1–2, 12, 18, 47–48), so he wisely inquires of the LORD (21:1a; see also 2:1; 5:19). David learns that the famine is due to the land being under a curse for a past sin of King Saul's, who broke Israel's covenant with the Gibeonites by shedding innocent blood (21:1b; Num. 35:33). When Israel entered the land they were told to exterminate the Canaanites (Deut. 20:16–18), but they were persuaded by the Gibeonites, who pretended to be from far away, to make a covenant of peace with them (Josh. 9:3–27). Saul, in his misguided zeal, had sought to exterminate the Gibeonites, in violation of the covenant Israel had made by oath (21:2). As a result, even though Saul is dead, his evil act brings judgment on the nation he once led. As the leader of Israel, King David accepts responsibility for the acts of his predecessor and humbles himself before the Gibeonites. He offers to make restitution (v. 3). The Gibeonites demand that seven of Saul's sons die to atone for his sin (vv. 4–6). David agrees and selects those who are to die, sparing Mephibosheth (vv. 7–8). These men then die an accursed death (v. 9; Deut. 21:22–23) in satisfaction of divine justice. In the aftermath, poor Rizpah tries to shield the bodies of her sons from further desecration (v. 10), and David gives Saul and his sons a proper burial (vv. 11–14a). After atonement is made, the LORD hears the king's prayer and again blesses the crops of his people (v. 14b; see also 24:25; 2 Chr. 7:14).

A passage like this baffles the modern mind. Some would say that this was barbaric.[1] It is implied that the act of killing Saul's sons somehow satisfies divine justice (21:6, 9, 14). Isn't it unjust for sons to die for the sins of their father (Deut. 24:16)? Is it possible that Saul's sons may have participated with their father in his evil act? As sinners they could not complain that they deserved better from God (Rom. 6:23). Perhaps the best explanation is that Saul sinned as a representative of his people, who then bore the consequences of his covenant breach.[2] Israel's leaders had sworn to protect the Gibeonites, and because Saul broke this covenant the nation suffered and Saul's family suffered. The fact that only seven died indicates that the LORD restrained His judgment upon Saul's house and upon the Israelites.

Ultimately, when we come to such a passage we must humble ourselves before God and His infallible Word (2 Tim. 3:16–17). There are hidden things which are hard for us to understand (Deut. 29:29). When we are tempted to question whether God is fair in a certain situation, we must acknowledge His goodness and justice, and submit to His sovereign will (Rom. 9:14–23).

The senseless census (24:1–25)

The last chapter of 2 Samuel has much in common with chapter 21. The people suffer for the sin of their king. When atonement is made, the LORD's wrath is turned away and the suffering ends. Chapter 24 provides even greater challenges for interpreters. While verse 1 says that *the LORD's anger* incited David to number Israel and Judah, the parallel text in 1 Chronicles 21:1 says that *Satan* moved David to number Israel. While some claim that this is a contradiction in Scripture, it actually exemplifies God's sovereignty over Satan and evil (Eph. 1:11; Rom. 8:28; Isa. 45:7). As is also taught in the book of Job, Satan cannot act without the LORD's permission (Job 1:6–12; 2:1–6). Satan's acts against Job are attributed as ultimately coming from the LORD (Job 2:3, 10). While God is never the Author of sin, He works out his perfect plan through agents who are opposed to Him, as is also seen in the cases of Joseph's brothers selling him as a slave, Pharaoh oppressing the Israelites, and, most importantly, the crucifixion of Jesus (Gen. 50:20; Exod. 9:16; Rom. 9:17; Acts 2:23; Isa. 53:10). So in the case of David numbering Israel, the LORD works through Satan to move David's heart to count the people as an occasion for bringing just judgment upon Israel. We are not told what Israel did to incite the LORD's anger, but we know that His anger is always just. We also know that the fact that God is sovereign over all things does not eliminate our responsibility and culpability for our sin (Isa. 10:5; Mark 14:21).

> The fact that God is sovereign over all things does not eliminate our responsibility and culpability for our sin.

One might also wonder what is wrong with taking a census. There were times in the past when the LORD commanded the leaders of Israel to number the people (Exod. 30:12; Num. 1–4). In this case, General Joab provides the most reasonable explanation for why David's act is evil. The king should trust in God and not be like the Gentile rulers, who trust in the size of their armies (vv. 2–3; 1 Chr. 21:3). "Some boast in chariots and some in horses, but we will boast in the name of the LORD, our God"; "The king is not saved by a mighty army ..." (Ps. 20:7; 33:16).

After Joab completes the census (v. 9), David's conscience is stricken and so he confesses his sin to the Lord (v. 10).[3] David seeks out the prophet Gad, and through Gad the LORD gives the king three options for the punishment for covenant disobedience to come upon Israel (vv. 11–13). Each potential punishment fits David's crime in that the great numbers of the people of Israel, of which David was so proud, are to be diminished. David throws himself upon the mercy of the LORD, who sends a terrible pestilence upon Israel in which tens of thousands are killed (vv. 15–16). David then intercedes for the people, and the LORD mercifully relents in the midst of judgment (v. 17). Now David is acting like a godly king who sees his people not merely as a means to make himself great, but as sheep for whom he should care. Perhaps this trial has done him good (Ps. 119:67, 71). David builds an altar and offers sacrifices to the LORD (vv. 18–24), whose anger is turned away by the king's intercession, and so He ends the plague (v. 25).

David's mighty men (21:15–22; 23:8–39)

In addition to the very difficult accounts in chapters 21 and 24, the epilogue to 2 Samuel also contains a record of the various exploits of David's mighty men. We are reminded that David is a great king who inspired great loyalty in men who were willing to stand with him in hard times and to risk their lives for him (23:13–17). We are also reminded that David did not achieve his victories alone. These mighty men, like David, fought for the LORD and gained their strength from Him (23:10, 12). Their exploits again illustrate how God sovereignly works through human effort and skill. The list of mighty men concludes with Uriah the Hittite (23:39), a sad reminder of David's great sin against God and against a loyal soldier whom he betrayed (1 Kings 15:5). Yet again we are reminded that only Christ is a perfect King.

Where do we see Jesus in this passage?

Just as the sins of Saul and David affected the people they represented, so when Adam, our representative, broke covenant with God he placed all his descendants under a deadly curse of death (Rom. 5:12). Jesus, the Son of God, bore the curse of our covenant disobedience on the cross, thus turning aside God's just anger against us (Rom. 5:18–19; Gal. 3:13; 2 Cor. 5:21). The blood atonement in these chapters reminds us how awful blood sacrifice is (Heb. 9:12, 22). Thanks be to God that, because Jesus intercedes for us, we will not die under God's curse (1 Tim. 2:5; Heb. 7:25)!

In looking upon his people as sheep (24:17) and making atonement so that God's wrath could be turned away (24:25), David is a picture of Christ, the Good Shepherd who laid down His life for His sheep (John 10:11). Jesus' costly (24:24) sacrifice turned away God's wrath (24:25; Rom. 3:25). It is also significant that the location at which David offered the sacrifice was the place where Abraham took Isaac to sacrifice him (Gen. 22) and the future site of the temple (2 Chr. 3:1), where sacrifices which foreshadowed Christ's death for us would be made to God.

Just as the mighty men risked their lives so that David could drink (23:15–17), so Jesus gave His life that we might drink. Just as David poured out the water, so Jesus poured out His life for us (Mark 14:24).

Just as the mighty men were called by God to serve alongside King David, so we are called to serve King Jesus by the strength the Lord gives as we participate in His victories (1 Peter 4:10–11; Rom. 8:37). We are also challenged by the example of the mighty men to be loyal to our King, even if His popularity wanes among the masses (Luke 22:28–29), and to be willing to give our lives for the One we love. He is worthy of our complete devotion (Rom. 12:1–2). You will never do as much for Him as He has already done for you.

How do these passages apply to us?

While there is no nation today which is in covenant with the LORD, He is still the Judge of the nations. Rulers are called by Him to enact justice by punishing evildoers and protecting those who do right (1 Peter 2:14). Just as many in Israel were affected by the sins of their rulers, so throughout history many have been afflicted because of the choices made by their political leaders, including millions who have died in famines and wars, and tens of millions of unborn babies who have died through abortion (Prov. 29:2; 28:12).

> While there is no nation today which is in covenant with the LORD, He is still the Judge of the nations.

The Scriptures teach that God is sovereign over disasters such as famines, earthquakes, tsunamis, and typhoons. "The One forming light and creating darkness, causing well-being and creating calamity; I am the LORD who does all these" (Isa. 45:7; see also Eph. 1:11). Unlike David (21:1), we may not know with certainty exactly why a certain calamity has occurred. We do know that because of the sin of our representative Adam, we live in a world under the curse of sin and death (Rom. 8:20; 6:23). The terrible calamities which take place are according to God's sovereign justice.

When we are afflicted by particular trials it is wise to ask if the LORD may be disciplining us for some particular area of sin in our lives (Heb. 12:4–11). We see from the example of Saul's sin against the Gibeonites that the LORD takes our commitments very seriously (Ps. 15:4; Matt. 5:31–37). It is astonishing how lightly many Christians take their promises in marriage and in commerce (e.g. debt). When we fail to keep our word, we and those under our care may experience the consequences.

We are also reminded that the LORD has a long memory and may choose to expose and punish sins, like that of Saul, from long ago (Num. 32:23). I knew a man who had a brief affair which he tried to keep secret. A long time after it was over, his wife received a letter from the other woman exposing everything. On the other hand, when we are wronged, we can trust God to bring justice, even if it doesn't occur as quickly as we would prefer (Rom. 12:19; Ps. 9:12).

We also are comforted by the fact that God uses our trials to help us to grow (James 1:2–4; Ps. 119:67, 71). Given that we are sinners who deserve everlasting death, we can never complain that the Lord is mistreating us (Rom. 6:23). As believers we rejoice that God has redeemed us from our sin, giving us life and a hope for a coming world in which there will be no more calamity and death (Rom. 8:18–25).

Just as David was tempted to take pride in the size of his armies, so nations today can be guilty of trusting in their military might. We can be tempted as individuals to trust in our savings or our job skills, rather than trusting in God. Churches which are growing numerically and prospering financially can be tempted to boast in themselves rather than in the LORD (Jer. 9:23–24).

One thing which sets David apart from other great men was his willingness to admit his sin (24:10, 17). Are you quick to confess your sin to God (1 John 1:8–10) and to man (Matt. 5:23–24)?

For further study ▶

FOR FURTHER STUDY

1. What was the significance under the Old Covenant of a famine in Israel?

2. How could Saul's descendants be justly punished for what their father did?

3. What do we learn from chapters 21 and 24 about interpreting difficult passages of Scripture?

4. Which of God's attributes are displayed in this section?

5. How do chapters 21 and 24 put King David in a favorable light?

6. Does the promise of 2 Chronicles 7:14 apply today? Why or why not?

7. How could David be blamed if the LORD incited him to number the people (24:1)?

8. Why did David pour out the water which his men risked their lives to get him (23:13–17)?

9. How does David serve as a type of Christ in this section?

TO THINK ABOUT AND DISCUSS

1. How do the actions of political leaders in our day bring harm to those under their authority?

2. Is there any such thing as a natural disaster (famine, earthquake, typhoon; Isa. 45:7)?

3. What does this section teach about the importance of keeping commitments?

4. Is it wrong for churches to keep statistics of finances and attendance? What dangers may lurk? What about Mark 6:44; 8:9; Acts 2:41; 4:4?

5. Are large numbers always a sign of God's blessing?

6. Are there lessons for older people to learn from David's retirement from battle (21:15–17)?

7. Who are Jesus' mighty men? What honor should be given to those who serve Christ?

8. How can we be like David's mighty men?

12 David's closing hymns

(22:1–23:7)

The centerpiece of the epilogue (chs. 21–24) contains two great psalms of David. The books of 1 and 2 Samuel, which were originally one work, begin with Hannah's song; then, near the conclusion of the Samuel narrative, we enjoy David's poetic masterpieces.

Hannah's song (1 Sam. 2:1–10) looks forward to God's great work which will take place through the anointed King David and ultimately Christ. David's psalms offer thanks to the LORD for His faithfulness in the past (22:1–51) and look forward with confidence to the future fulfillment of His great promises (23:1–7). Both Hannah's song and the songs of David poetically summarize key teachings of 1 and 2 Samuel. They use similar vocabulary (horn, enemies, salvation, rock, bows) and both speak of the LORD's anointed king who delivers His people (1 Sam. 2:10; 2 Sam. 22:51; 23:1). What Hannah anticipated many years before is fulfilled in an immediate sense through David, who delivers Israel from the dark, oppressive days of the judges. Both Hannah and David look forward to the final fulfillment in Jesus, the anointed Son of David who will reign forever (22:51).

A royal psalm of thanksgiving for the Lord's past faithfulness (22:1–51)

Second Samuel 22 follows the pattern of a royal psalm of thanksgiving. There is an introductory summary, then the psalmist recalls a crisis, he calls upon the Lord, the Lord delivers him, and finally David expresses gratitude for all that the Lord has done for him. Unlike most psalms of thanksgiving which recall a particular deliverance, this psalm of David recalls a lifetime of deliverances. This psalm is almost identical to Psalm 18 and is the longest of the psalms specifically attributable to David.

This psalm can, in a sense, be sung in three-part harmony. David sings of his own life experience. We can also sing about how the Lord delivers us. And this psalm could be sung by Jesus. Some parts of the psalm are only completely true of Christ: "The Lord has rewarded me according to my righteousness; according to the cleanness of my hands He has recompensed me. For I have kept the ways of the Lord, and have not acted wickedly against My God" (vv. 21–22).

In the summary of praise David recalls that the Lord is a great Savior. It is appropriate that the song which summarizes David's illustrious life gives glory to the Lord, rather than merely extolling Israel's greatest king (v. 1). David is unique among the kings of the nations, and even among the kings of Israel, in that he honors the Lord above himself. He offers a nine-fold description of the greatness of the Lord (vv. 2–3).

What David sings of the LORD is later sung about Jesus. God has raised up a powerful horn of salvation for His people (Luke 1:68–69). We too can sing of how God has delivered us through our great King.

David then recalls the terrible troubles he experienced (vv. 5–6), which could refer to times when he fled from Saul, or when he faced the Philistines. Jesus also experienced great suffering and distress. "My soul has become troubled; and what shall I say, 'Father, save Me from this hour?' But for this purpose I came to this hour" (John 12:27; see also Luke 22:44). As followers of Jesus we also experience afflictions in this life. "Many are the afflictions of the righteous, but the LORD delivers him out of them all" (Ps. 34:19; see also 1 Peter 4:12; 2 Tim. 3:12). Just as David called out to the LORD in his distress (v. 7), so Jesus cried out to His Father in the midst of His suffering (Heb. 5:7–8; Matt. 26:38–39; 27:46). We also are invited to call upon Him in our distress. "Call upon Me in the day of trouble; I shall rescue you, and you will honor me" (Ps. 50:15; see also 1 Peter 5:7).

David remembers how the LORD answered his cries, shaking heaven and earth as He rushed to his aid (vv. 8–16). Similarly, nature was literally in tumult when Jesus came to deliver us. The heavens were affected by His coming (Matt. 2:2) and the earth was darkened and shaken at His death (Matt. 27:45, 51–54; 28:2). When He returns for our final deliverance, there will be disturbances both in the heavens and on earth (Matt. 24:29–31). Because of Christ we are assured that the LORD hears and helps us when we are distressed (Matt. 7:7).

The LORD, on many occasions, delivered David from his

enemies (vv. 17–20a). Jesus was not abandoned to Sheol (the grave), but was raised from the dead and exalted to the Father's right hand (Acts 2:24–36). God also intervenes in our lives, delivering us from darkness and death through the gospel.

David declares that the LORD's deliverance came as a reward for his righteous obedience (vv. 20b–25). We might wonder how this could be true in light of his great sin with Bathsheba. What makes David stand out from other kings, though, is that when he sinned, he humbly repented (12:13; 24:10, 17; Ps. 32; 51). Furthermore, though his life was not perfect, it was characterized by obedience to God: "David did what was right in the sight of the LORD, and had not turned aside from anything that He commanded him all the days of his life, except in the case of Uriah the Hittite" (1 Kings 15:5). But only Jesus can say, without any qualification, that He has been rewarded according to His righteousness (Ps. 24:3–5). The Father delights in Him because Jesus always did the Father's will and never sinned (Isa. 42:1; Luke 3:22; Matt. 27:43; 1 Peter 1:19; Heb. 4:15; Acts 2:33; Rom. 1:4). He was rewarded according to the merit of His perfect righteousness. In what sense can we sing these words (vv. 20b–25)? The LORD rewards us with salvation because of what Jesus has accomplished for us. His righteousness is counted as ours by grace through faith (Rom. 5:19; 1 Peter 3:18; Phil. 3:9). David too needed the grace and forgiveness which comes through Christ (Rom. 4:6–8).

> **What makes David stand out from other kings is that when he sinned, he humbly repented.**

Yet it is also true that those who follow Christ should live lives characterized by holy obedience which springs from His work in our lives (Titus 2:11–15). There is a God-pleasing practical righteousness which characterizes true believers in whose lives the Holy Spirit is working (Luke 1:5–6; 2:25; 23:50; Matt. 1:19; John 14:15). God blesses and honors the practical moral obedience of His people (1 Peter 3:12; Heb. 6:10). Even our good works are the result of His work in us (Eph. 2:10).

David goes on to declare that the LORD always deals justly with mankind and has a special care for the afflicted (vv. 26–28). David remembers the LORD's special care for him (vv. 29–30).

In the next major section David recalls how the Lord who is great and worthy of praise (vv. 31–33) has given him total victory over his enemies, both foreign and domestic, so that now he is a great king among the nations (vv. 34–46; see also Deut. 33:28; Ps. 2:8–12). Jesus too has triumphed over His enemies, through the cross (1 John 3:8; Col. 2:15). He has crushed the serpent's head (v. 43; Gen. 3:15). He is now exalted over the nations (vv. 45–46; Phil. 2:9–11). We too can sing of the LORD delivering us (Isa. 40:28–31). We have terrible and strong enemies (1 Peter 5:8), but the LORD has strengthened us for battle and gives us victory (Eph. 6:10–13; Rom. 16:20).

This psalm closes with a summarizing doxology of praise to the LORD (vv. 47–51). The LORD is a Rock of strength and salvation for His people. He is worthy of our praise. Jesus fulfilled the hope of David by bringing deliverance and establishing an everlasting kingdom. The nations will praise

God because of His work (v. 50; Rom. 15:9–12). We too praise God for His gracious dealings with us (Ps. 34:19).

David looks forward to the coming of the royal Messiah (23:1–7)

David's last recorded words are both poetic and prophetic. As he is in the valley of the shadow of death, he looks forward to the coming of the Messiah. After recalling how the LORD has elevated him, David continues to speak by divine inspiration (vv. 1–3a). David is a great king, but he anticipates a future King who will rule in perfect righteousness and will bring great blessing to His subjects (vv. 3b–4). This King will fulfill all the LORD's covenant promises to David and to Israel (v. 5; 7:11–16). He will judge those who defy the LORD (vv. 6–7). The faithful in future generations will rely upon this promise (Isa. 9:6–7; Jer. 23:5–6; Ezek. 34:23–24). We read David's words with great personal joy because the righteous Messianic King (the Son of David) whom David anticipated has come (Matt. 1:1, 20; 9:27; 12:23; Luke 1:27, 32, 69; 2:4, 11; Rom. 1:3; Rev. 22:16). Jesus, like David, had a lowly earthly beginning from which He has been exalted (22:1b; Luke 2:7; Phil. 2:5–8). He was anointed by God (23:1c; Acts 4:27). He is the perfect Ruler who fulfills the yearning of God's people for a righteous King who will bring prosperity to His people (vv. 4–5; Heb. 1:9 Isa. 11:1–5). He will also justly destroy God's enemies with fire (vv. 6–7; Matt. 13:30, 40–42).

FOR FURTHER STUDY

1. Why are these psalms placed at the end of 2 Samuel?

2. How do these psalms compare to Hannah's song at the beginning of 1 Samuel?

3. Why does God speak to us through psalms?

4. In light of David's great sin, how could he say that the LORD had rewarded him according to his *righteousness* (22:21–24)?

5. List several of God's attributes which are praised in these psalms.

6. How does Jesus fulfill Israel's expectation for the Messianic King (23:1–7)?

TO THINK ABOUT AND DISCUSS

1. How could these psalms be sung by David, by Jesus, and by you?

2. In what ways does the LORD reward us according to righteousness (22:21–24)?

3. If it is the LORD who gives victory, why did David have to fight so hard in battle? By what means does the LORD give us victory?

4. Compose a psalm of praise to God for His faithfulness to you.

5. Second Samuel 23:1–7 contains David's last words. What would you want your last words to be?

Conclusion

David was a great king by whom all future kings of Israel would be measured. By faith in the LORD he won great victories and elevated Israel among the nations. He was not perfect, but he was willing to confess his sins. Sadly, as 1 and 2 Kings record, the nation of Israel would never again have a king as great as David in the Old Covenant era.

David's greatness points to Christ, who exhibits all David's strengths with perfection. David's sin reminds us that we need a greater king than David. For many centuries, Israel went from bad to worse, until the day when angels announced in the city of David that the longed-for Son of David had come. Through Him, all the LORD's promises to David were fulfilled (Luke 2:11). Though David grew old and weary so that he was unable to go to battle (21:15–17) and then finally died, our Savior lives and will reign on the throne of David forever (7:16; Rev. 11:15).

Endnotes

Chapter 1

1   A great miscalculation in light of what happens to him. Is the messenger even telling the truth (1 Sam. 31:5–6)?

2   Also see 3:26–30; 4:9–12; and 18:19–33 for unexpected responses to news.

3   Given that one of David's wives was Jonathan's sister Michal, who placed little value on the things of God (6:20–23), we can see how a faithful godly friend like Jonathan would, in contrast, be greatly valued.

Chapter 2

1   The scene may have been like that in University Baptist Church, Waco, Texas, when in October 2005 a microphone fell into the baptistery, electrocuting and killing Pastor Kyle Lake—though Pastor Lake had done no wrong.

Chapter 4

1   David had also sworn to Saul that he would not wipe out his family (1 Sam. 24:20–23).

2   Later it will be suggested that Mephibosheth has ambitions to be king (16:3).

Chapter 5

1   In some cases, their husbands were subordinates to the offending pastor, just as Uriah was to David.

2   James also warns us not to blame God when we are tempted (James 1:13).

3   With guardrails for safety— Deuteronomy 22:8.

4   It is ironic that Bathsheba was concerned about outward ceremonial cleanness after committing adultery (v. 4).

5   Joab, by being useful to David in this situation, also secures his own position and gains future leverage over David.

6   The fourth commandment (Exod. 20:8–11) not only tells us to rest on the Sabbath, but also instructs us to work for six days. David, by not pursuing his vocation as the leader of the

army of Israel, was in violation of this commandment.

Chapter 6

1 Such parables are used in both the Old and the New Testaments (2 Sam. 14:1–20; Isa. 5:17; Ezek. 17:2–10; Matt. 13:3; etc.).

Chapter 7

1 It has been said that one reason why rapists hate their victims is because even in their evil act they experience rejection. They can only get what they want by brute force, reminding themselves of their inadequacy.

2 The word used of Amnon putting her out is also used of divorce in Deuteronomy 24:1.

3 There are also parallels between Absalom's act of revenge and the account in Genesis 34 of Jacob's sons avenging the violation of their sister Dinah. Jacob, like David, had failed to act so his sons took matters into their own hands. They gained the trust of the Shechemites and through deceit made them vulnerable to attack, thus taking their bloody revenge. We are also reminded of the very first murder, that of Abel by Cain, which was also fratricide and which happened when they were away from the family and then led to Cain's estrangement from the clan (Gen. 4:8, 12).

4 Steve Viars, *Putting Your Past in Its Place: Moving Forward in Freedom and Forgiveness* (Eugene, OR: Harvest House, 2011).

5 Matthew Henry, *Commentary on the Whole Bible,* vol. ii: Joshua to Esther (Iowa Falls, IA: World Bible Publishers, [n.d.]), p. 507.

6 Ibid.

7 See Jim Newheiser and Elyse Fitzpatrick, *You Never Stop Being a Parent: Thriving in Relationship with Your Adult Children* (Phillipsburg, NJ: P & R, 2010).

8 The following two books are strongly recommended for

victims of sexual abuse: Justin S. Holcomb and Lindsey A. Holcomb, *Rid of My Disgrace: Hope and Healing for Victims of Sexual Assault* (Wheaton, IL: Crossway, 2011); Robert W. Kellermen, *Sexual Abuse: Beauty for Ashes* (Phillipsburg, PA: P & R, 2013).

Chapter 8

1 David refuses to use the ark of God as a talisman in battle (1 Sam. 4).
2 Perhaps because Ahithophel was Bathsheba's grandfather (2 Sam. 23:34; 11:3).
3 Shimei did deserve punishment for cursing the LORD's anointed ruler (Exod. 22:28).

Chapter 9

1 This is like a game of chess where you aren't allowed to attack the other side's king. You can't win!
2 War itself is an exceptional situation when it comes to the taking of life (Exod. 20:13; Rom. 13:4).

3 The one time in my life which might have qualified was when I was being interrogated by an official in an Islamic country in which Christian worship is illegal and I refused to offer the official the truth about who was involved in our underground Christian fellowship.
4 C. H. Spurgeon, *The Metropolitan Tabernacle Pulpit: Sermons Preached and Revised*, vol. xxiv (London: Passmore & Alabaster, 1879), p. 508.

Chapter 10

1 Killing Absalom was also in the king's interest.
2 Later, when David is about to die, he encourages Solomon to find a way to punish Shimei (1 Kings 2:8–9, 36–46).
3 We, like Chimham, are blessed because of the faithfulness of another (19:37, 40; 2 Cor. 5:21).

Chapter 11

1 Ironically, many of the people who would condemn this

passage of Scripture are unmoved by the millions of unborn babies who die every year.

2   Later, 70,000 die because of David's sin (24:15).

3   Again, it takes David several months to acknowledge his guilt, but at least this time he doesn't need Nathan the prophet to confront him (2 Sam. 12).

Additional resources

Commentaries on 2 Samuel

Davis, Dale Ralph, *2 Samuel: Out of Every Adversity* (Fearn: Christian Focus, 2008)

Keddie, Gordon J., *Triumph of the King: The Message of 2 Samuel* (Durham: Evangelical Press, 1990)

Audio sermons on 2 Samuel

The Web site of Grace Bible Church, Escondido, CA (www.grcbible.org) contains audios and outlines preached by the author on 2 Samuel.